Letts

KT-149-235

GCSE

VISUAL REVISION GUIDE

SUCCESS

ENGLISH AND ENGLISH LITERATURE

Authors

Frank Fitzsimons and John Mannion

CONTENTS

PUNCTUATION AND SPEAKING AND LISTENING

WRITING AND THE MEDIA

SHAKESPEARE

POETRY

NOVELS AND SHORT STORIES

WHAT YOU NEED TO KNOW ABOUT ENGLISH AND ENGLISH LITERATURE AT GCSE

It is important to know what is expected of you. This page shows you how your course is structured, how to begin your revision and where you can find ideas for catch-up assignments. First of all, you need to realise that although you go to 'English' lessons at school, you are likely to be studying for two exams – English and English Literature.

ENGLISH

In English, <u>coursework</u> accounts for 40% of your final grade.
• 20% for <u>Speaking and Listening</u>   • 20% for <u>Reading and Writing</u>
In English Literature, <u>coursework</u> accounts for 30% of your grade.
The good news is that for some units you are allowed to submit the same coursework for both exams. These are called '<u>crossover units</u>'.
For your English exam you will be assessed in the following areas:

SPEAKING AND LISTENING (EN1)

There are <u>three oral assessments:</u> single, pair work and group.
The marks are added and then divided by three for the final mark. It is worth doing as many orals as you can. The best in each category can then be submitted as your mark.

There are two <u>coursework</u> responses to <u>Reading</u> (EN2) and two responses to <u>Writing</u> (EN3):
• Shakespeare (EN2)* (5%)
• Prose Study (EN2)* (5%)
• Media (EN3 analyse, review, comment) (5%)
• Original Writing (EN3 imagine, explore, entertain) (5%)
* = crossover assignments
<u>Notice that the two EN2 assignments are crossover assignments. This means that they will get you a literature mark as well.</u>

<u>Shakespeare</u> – There is no set play so the one you study will depend on your teacher's choice.

<u>Prose study</u> – If it is to be a crossover assignment, the text you study must have been written <u>before 1914</u> by an author recognised within <u>The National Curriculum</u>. There is a wider choice if it is not used as a crossover.

<u>Media</u> – This assignment can range from a comparative analysis of two soap operas from different countries to an analysis of an advert. The media assignment is considered as <u>both a reading and a writing assignment.</u>

<u>Original Writing</u> – Here you may write <u>fiction</u>, such as a story or a number of poems, or <u>non-fiction</u>, such as an autobiography.

EXAMS ACCOUNT FOR 60% OF YOUR GRADE

READING (EN2)
<u>Unseen</u>
Media and non-fiction texts 15%

<u>Prepared Texts</u>
Poems from different cultures 15%

WRITING (EN3)
Writing to advise, inform, explain or describe 15%

ENGLISH LITERATURE

Coursework accounts for 30% of the final grade.
Pre-1914 Drama – Shakespeare* 10%
Pre-1914 Prose* 10%, Post-1914 Drama 10%

Only the post-1914 drama coursework is not crossover.

EXAMS ACCOUNT FOR 70% OF YOUR GRADE

Set texts – 30%
Poems in the English literary heritage – 40%

Examiner's Top Tip
Try answering questions against the clock – some questions give you only 30 minutes. You will find suggestions for exam practice in the exam sections of this book.

HOW TO BEGIN YOUR REVISION

WHAT YOU NEED TO KNOW ABOUT ENGLISH AT GCSE

✔ <u>KNOW</u> <u>YOUR</u> <u>COURSE</u> <u>REQUIREMENTS</u>. If you know what the requirements of the course are then you will stand a much better chance of meeting them. Make sure that you understand how your course is set out. <u>Ask</u> <u>your</u> <u>teacher</u> <u>for</u> <u>advice</u> on what you can expect to face in your exams. Look at past exam papers fairly early in your course, as these will help you understand what you have to aim for to get a good mark.

✔ <u>COMPLETE</u> <u>YOUR</u> <u>COURSEWORK</u>. You <u>cannot</u> <u>get</u> <u>a</u> <u>good</u> <u>grade</u> <u>unless</u> <u>all</u> <u>your</u> <u>coursework</u> <u>is</u> <u>completed</u>. If you have worked steadily throughout the two-year course you should be fine. You can always submit new assignments to get better grades, providing that you are not overdoing it by racing to catch up with your course-work in several subjects. If you fall behind with your assignments, you risk producing poor ones by rushing them.

Examiner's Top Tip
Revise all aspects of punctuation early in your course because this will help you to produce better course-work and it will also give you more confidence for your final exams.

✔ <u>PRODUCE</u> <u>A</u> <u>REVISION</u> <u>TIMETABLE</u>. Time management is crucial at every stage in your revision, not just in the exams themselves. You will relieve the pressure on yourself if you <u>manage</u> <u>your</u> <u>time</u> <u>properly</u>, allotting time to every part of the exam.
- Leave yourself time to <u>relax</u> and do not overdo it! If you try <u>too</u> hard, you could end up doing your best work outside the exam room because you are <u>too</u> tired and stale.
- <u>Go</u> <u>to</u> <u>bed</u> in good time and do not be tempted to stay up late doing last-minute revision.
- Allow a few days in your revision timetable in which you do <u>nothing</u> <u>at</u> <u>all</u>. You will recharge your batteries and be the better for it. Again, if you do not understand something, have a <u>short</u> <u>break</u> and <u>return</u> <u>to</u> <u>the</u> <u>problem</u> <u>later</u> <u>on</u>. This works because your brain is still unconsciously puzzling things out while you are doing something else. When you start your revision again the problem may seem <u>simple</u> <u>to</u> <u>solve</u>.

✔ <u>STICK</u> <u>WITH</u> <u>IT</u>. A <u>little</u> <u>and</u> <u>often</u> is better for the mind than doing a lot, rarely. That is how people learn foreign languages.

✔ <u>BE</u> <u>CONFIDENT</u>. If you have done <u>everything</u> <u>possible</u> during your revision you should then be able to give a good account of yourself. Go into the exam hall with the idea of <u>doing</u> <u>yourself</u> <u>justice</u>! Show examiners what you know but remember to <u>keep</u> <u>your</u> <u>points</u> <u>relevant</u>. You will probably only use a fraction of what you know in the exam, which is why it is important to be <u>selective</u> in how you present your ideas.

✔ <u>BEGIN</u> <u>NOW</u>. Pair up with a friend if this helps to <u>motivate</u> you. You can divide up the work and report your findings to each other. Why not <u>proof-read</u> <u>each</u> <u>other's</u> <u>work</u>? You will get better at spotting your mistakes.

CATCHING UP ON MISSING ASSIGNMENTS OR PRODUCING BETTER ONES

It is easy to <u>miss</u> <u>an</u> <u>assignment</u> or leave it <u>so</u> <u>late</u> that another one gets in the way. Maybe you are dissatisfied with a coursework assignment that you rushed. Perhaps you thought that you could have done a better one.

In each of the coursework sections that follow at least <u>one</u> <u>alternative</u> <u>catch-up</u> <u>assignment</u> will be suggested. If you use an idea from this book for a catch-up assignment, remember to <u>clear</u> <u>it</u> <u>with</u> <u>your</u> <u>teacher</u> <u>first</u>. Your teacher is the one who has to submit your coursework to the exam board and do all the paperwork.

PUNCTUATION AGAIN!

- **Why? You may be still surviving on skills learned in Year 8.**
- **You cannot get good grades in English Language unless you can punctuate your writing skilfully and correctly.**

WHY USE PUNCTUATION?

- **When you speak,** you punctuate naturally through your pauses and body language. However, <u>when you write you have to help your reader understand what you mean through a variety of punctuation marks.</u> The more you know about punctuation the better you will be able to express yourself. Pupils who use <u>semi-colons and colons</u> stand out from others, especially if they use these punctuation marks effectively.

- **Writing** is a <u>second-hand way of getting our meaning across</u> to others; we need to punctuate our work to help our audience understand us. Remember that when we let our writing pass into the hands of others, our punctuation marks and the words we use to express ourselves are all that there is to communicate our message. We are no longer in a position to put right any errors, as we would be if we were speaking directly to our audience.

punctuation marks

- **To sum up:** we use punctuation marks to <u>clarify</u> the points and ideas that we want to communicate to others.

INTERNET
Have a look at this for info on punctuation:
http://www.http://www3.open.ac.uk/learners-guide/
learning-skills/english/sect5/punctuation.htm

Examiner's Top Tip
Markers can miss good points and ideas in your writing when their attention is continually drawn to punctuation errors.

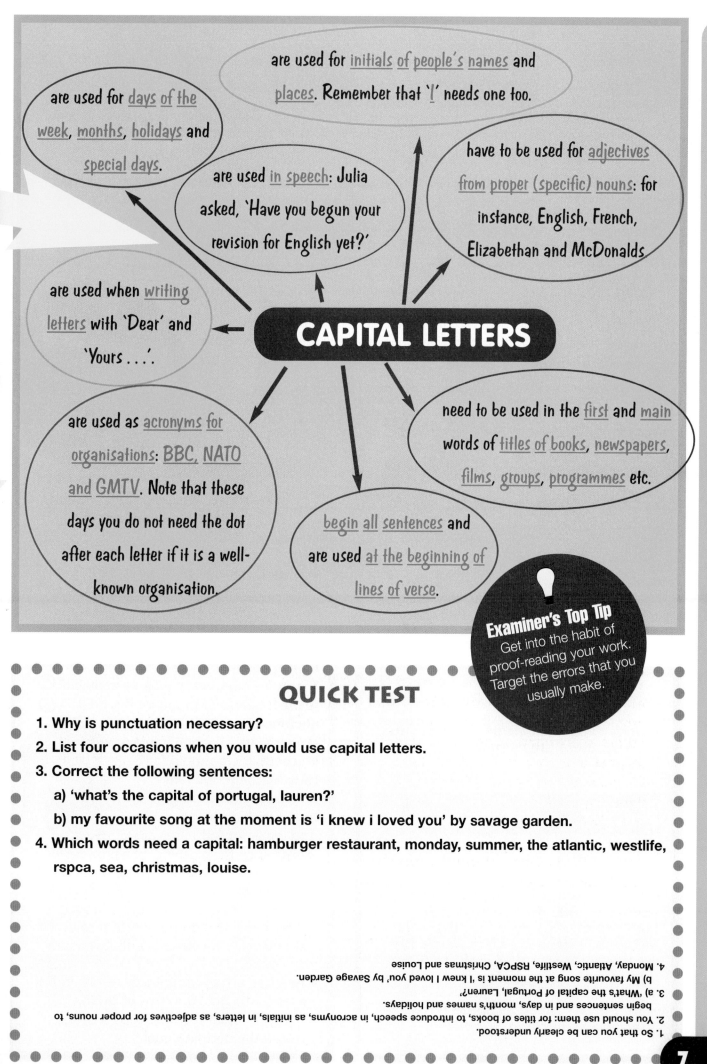

CAPITAL LETTERS

are used for <u>initials</u> <u>of</u> <u>people's</u> <u>names</u> and <u>places</u>. Remember that '<u>I</u>' needs one too.

are used for <u>days</u> <u>of</u> <u>the</u> <u>week</u>, <u>months</u>, <u>holidays</u> and <u>special</u> <u>days</u>.

are used <u>in</u> <u>speech</u>: Julia asked, 'Have you begun your revision for English yet?'

have to be used for <u>adjectives</u> <u>from</u> <u>proper</u> (specific) <u>nouns</u>: for instance, English, French, Elizabethan and McDonalds

are used when <u>writing</u> <u>letters</u> with 'Dear' and 'Yours . . .'.

are used as <u>acronyms</u> <u>for</u> <u>organisations</u>: BBC, NATO and GMTV. Note that these days you do not need the dot after each letter if it is a well-known organisation.

<u>begin</u> <u>all</u> <u>sentences</u> and are used <u>at</u> <u>the</u> <u>beginning</u> <u>of</u> <u>lines</u> <u>of</u> <u>verse</u>.

need to be used in the <u>first</u> and <u>main</u> words of <u>titles</u> <u>of</u> <u>books</u>, <u>newspapers</u>, <u>films</u>, <u>groups</u>, <u>programmes</u> etc.

Examiner's Top Tip
Get into the habit of proof-reading your work. Target the errors that you usually make.

QUICK TEST

1. Why is punctuation necessary?
2. List four occasions when you would use capital letters.
3. Correct the following sentences:
   a) 'what's the capital of portugal, lauren?'
   b) my favourite song at the moment is 'i knew i loved you' by savage garden.
4. Which words need a capital: hamburger restaurant, monday, summer, the atlantic, westlife, rspca, sea, christmas, louise.

4. Monday, Atlantic, Westlife, RSPCA, Christmas and Louise
b) My favourite song at the moment is 'I knew I loved you' by Savage Garden.
3. a) 'What's the capital of Portugal, Lauren?'
begin sentences and in days, month's names and holidays.
2. You should use them: for titles of books, to introduce speech, in acronyms, as initials, in letters, as adjectives for proper nouns, to
1. So that you can be clearly understood.

FULL STOPS

This is the main punctuation mark that signals the <u>end</u> <u>of</u> <u>one</u> <u>idea</u> <u>and</u> <u>the</u> <u>beginning</u> <u>of</u> <u>another</u>. Sentences help complete ideas in your writing. Use full stops to make <u>strong</u> <u>points</u> in your writing as they slow readers down. If you want your readers to mull over what you have to say or if you have an important point to make, use a full stop. If you want your readers to read your ideas quickly, use <u>semi-colons</u> or <u>colons</u>.

To get high grades in GCSE you will need to <u>vary</u> <u>the</u> <u>length</u> <u>of</u> <u>your</u> <u>sentences</u> and the <u>style</u> of your punctuation.

<u>Change</u> <u>your</u> <u>sentences</u> <u>by</u> <u>making</u> <u>some</u> <u>long</u> <u>and</u> <u>some</u> <u>short</u>; variety is the spice of life and your task is to keep your audience interested in what you want to say. You can add to the variety by using a range of <u>connective</u> words that will also give you a range of <u>expressive</u> possibilities. Try to be expressive through your choice of punctuation. If you want to describe something use <u>semi-colons</u>; if you want to make effective <u>statements</u> and <u>commands</u> use <u>full</u> <u>stops</u>.

Read your work aloud and listen to where one idea ends and another begins. Each idea is a sentence. Trust your ears.

Examiner's Top Tip
Select the punctuation mark that best fits the meaning and purpose. The more expressive you are the better your writing will be.

SEMI-COLONS

<u>Semi-colons</u> <u>have</u> <u>many</u> <u>uses</u>.

- **They join two or more closely related ideas:**

1. **Steve worked hard for his results; he stuck to his revision plan.**
2. **Spring has come early; the trees have begun to blossom and the grassy banks are full of daffodils.**
3. **There are a number of good movies on tonight; just after the news on ITV they are showing _Clueless_.**

- **They separate sets of items in a list when there are commas within the sets or lists:**

When you unpack your new computer and set it up you should follow the loose-leaf instructions packed with your computer; you will then, if you look carefully, find everything you need: multi-coloured leads; the plugs for your monitor and base unit; the speakers with their leads; a microphone, if this is included, with a stand; manuals for your computer and, if you are lucky, lots of interesting software.

- **You do not need a capital letter after a semi-colon.**

COLONS

These are two dots, one above the other, and they signify a new sentence. They are used to:

⇢introduce a list:
You should bring to your exam: a watch, two pens, a pencil and a ruler, tissues and hope!
⇢introduce quotations:
Hamlet ponders: 'To be or not to be. That is the question.' It is also acceptable to use a comma to introduce this brief quotation from 'Hamlet'.
⇢punctuate dialogue in plays:
Macbeth: If we should fail?
Lady Macbeth: We fail!
But screw your courage
to the sticking place,
And we'll not fail.
⇢expand on the meaning of a previous idea:
Tracy scored the highest grade in the exam: it was an A*.

A dash can also do the job of a colon by emphasising the sentence that follows:

- Tom had achieved fantastic results in his exams – he got As in five of them.
- The girls' team won the cup – Phyllis scored the deciding goal.

OTHER PUNCTUATION

EXCLAMATION MARKS
These marks help express surprise, anger, fear, joy and most other emotions. For instance: Louise! It is good to see you!

QUESTION MARKS
These marks can be used for <u>rhetorical</u> <u>questions</u> where no direct reply is expected, only mental agreement: 'Who could defend a statement like that?'. <u>They</u> <u>can</u> <u>also</u> <u>be</u> <u>used</u> <u>for</u> <u>requests</u> <u>for</u> <u>information</u>: 'What time is it?' You do not need a question mark for an <u>indirect</u> <u>question</u>: 'Siobhan asked me for a pen.'

Five Things to Remember
1. All sentences need punctuation marks to show that they have ended.
2. To get the highest grades in GCSE English you will have to use a wide range of punctuation.
3. Vary the length and style of your sentences to maintain the interest of your audience.
4. Look carefully at how professional writers and authors punctuate their work and try to work out the effects the writers are aiming to produce.
5. If you do not punctuate your work properly, you risk being misunderstood.

PUNCTUATION THAT MARKS THE END OF A SENTENCE

Punctuation helps you express yourself clearly so that you can get your ideas across to others.

QUICK TEST

1. Which are the quickest to get through when reading: full stops or semi-colons?
2. Explain one of the things that semi-colons can do.
3. What is a sentence?
4. Can a colon introduce a list of items?
5. Can colons be used to introduce a quotation?
6. Give one other purpose for a colon.

Examiner's Top Tip
Look at how professional writers use punctuation as you read their work. Pause over some passages and think about the effectiveness of the punctuation.

1. Semi-colons
2. They link two closely related phrases or separate sets of items in a list where there are commas within the sets.
3. It usually expresses a single idea.
4. Yes
5. Yes
6. It links another phrase which expands upon the meaning of the first, or punctuates dialogue in plays.

SPEECH, QUOTATION AND TITLE MARKS AND COMMAS

Examiner's Top Tip
We use commas, naturally, when we speak but be careful not use them instead of full stops in sentences.

The skilful use of punctuation marks can improve your expression.

COMMAS

Commas have a variety of uses.

They can be used to <u>separate</u> <u>items</u> <u>in</u> <u>lists</u>: I would like three hamburgers, a cheeseburger, a large serving of fries and a coffee.

They are used to <u>clarify</u> <u>sentences</u> that could be misleading: After a period of calm, students returned after the fire alarm.

They need to be used in <u>direct</u> <u>speech</u>: Elaine was curious about the previous evening and asked, 'Where did you get to?'
'The shopping centre,' John replied.

They can be used to mark off <u>words</u>, <u>phrases</u>, and <u>connectives</u> in sentences: Billy, who did not like to be made fun of, was angry. On the other hand, there was no harm in what Carly said.

Examiner's Top Tip
Whether you use double inverted commas or single ones in your direct speech – be consistent.

SPEECH, QUOTATION AND TITLE MARKS

SPEECH

There are four main rules for setting out speech:

1. Use <u>inverted</u> <u>commas</u> for the words spoken: Catherine said, 'I haven't seen you in ages!'
2. <u>Direct</u> <u>speech</u> must be separated from the rest of the writing by a punctuation mark. See the comma in the example above.
3. Remember to use a <u>capital</u> <u>letter</u> when you begin the direct speech: Catherine said, 'It's ages since I last saw you.'
4. Each time you introduce a <u>new</u> <u>speaker</u> begin a <u>new</u> <u>line</u> and <u>indent</u>. That is, begin the speech of your new speaker three letter spaces to the right of the margin.

QUOTATION MARKS

- These are inverted commas for words or phrases cited from texts. Stick with single inverted commas for speech and double inverted commas for speech within speech. For instance: Jane shouted to her husband in the next room, 'Your mother phoned and she said, "When are you going to visit me?" Colin, I thought that you called in on her last week.'

- <u>Remember</u> <u>to</u> <u>close</u> <u>them</u>. It is confusing for readers and markers if you fail to do so! To show that you are ending a quotation, place the final full stop on the outside of the inverted comma as with the following example. In My Fair Lady Eliza Doolittle shows her independence from Professor Higgins when she says, 'I can do without you'.

TITLE MARKS

- In secondary schools inverted commas are used to signify: book titles, stories, newspapers, magazines, television programmes, movies or shows. For example, 'My Fair Lady' is the title of the musical or 1964 film version of the play, 'Pygmalion'.

- In your writing always use title marks to show the difference between eponymous characters and the names of the plays and novels in which they appear: Macbeth is a character whereas 'Macbeth' is a play. (Eponymous characters share their name with the titles of their texts.)

- The convention (or accepted rule) for titles in universities is to underline them: <u>Hamlet</u> and <u>Macbeth</u>. The main thing is to remain consistent in your method of identifying titles.

- Note that if you use italics for titles then this is acceptable for printed work. Notice that in much of this book italics have been used for the titles of texts and films.

QUICK TEST

1. Identify three uses for commas.
2. Write a sentence in which you need an exclamation mark.
3. Do you need a question mark for indirect or reported speech?
4. Make up a sentence in which you use all four rules for setting out speech.
5. What do you need to use when you write out the title of a film, book, story, etc. ?

1. They can mark off a list and phrases within a sentence. They are also used within direct speech.
2. Good Heavens!
3. No
4. Phil said, 'Buy the latest team shirt.'
   'It is too expensive,' said Paul.
5. Either title marks, underlining or italics

APOSTROPHES OF POSSESSION AND CONTRACTION

They help shorten words or show that something belongs to someone.

Examiner's Top Tip
Abbreviated words are to be used only in informal writing. We use them when we speak or write to friends or family. Avoid using shortened words in your assignments and exams unless you are asked to do so.

Key Fact

<u>Its and it's can be confusing words</u>. If you wrote, 'I emptied a box of its contents', you would not need an apostrophe. This is because 'its' in this instance is a possessive pronoun. On the other hand if you say, 'It's going to rain all day', you need an apostrophe because you mean 'it is'.

APOSTROPHES THAT SHOW POSSESSION

POSSESSIVE PRONOUNS
<u>Pronouns like these do not need apostrophes to show ownership</u>:
• my
• his
• hers
• yours
• its
• ours
• theirs

EXAMPLES
The computer is hers.
The watch is mine.
The house is theirs.
The bag is yours.

APOSTROPHES OF OWNERSHIP FOR ONE PERSON OR THING
If there is a <u>**single**</u> owner, place the apostrophe <u>**before**</u> the 's':
• Tim's video player
• Christine's house
• The sun's rays

APOSTROPHES OF OWNERSHIP FOR MORE THAN ONE OWNER
If there is <u>**more than one**</u> owner, you need to put the apostrophe <u>**after**</u> the 's' to show that you mean a <u>**plural**</u> owner:
• The Jacksons' video
• The Smiths' house

<u>If a person's name naturally ends in 's' you can do one of two things</u>:
• James's haircut
or
• James' haircut
• The Jones's house
Whichever style you go for, stick with it because readers and markers like you to remain consistent.

If a plural noun does <u>**not**</u> need an 's' to make it plural, you should place your apostrophe <u>**before**</u> the 's':
• The men's business venture
• The women's society
• The children's playground
• The people's champion

EXPRESSION
You can vary your expression by using an apostrophe:
• 'The claws of the cat' becomes 'The cat's claws' with an apostrophe.
If you are unsure of where to put a possessive apostrophe then write your sentence the long way round:
• 'Dan's new house' becomes 'The new house of Dan'.
Always ask yourself why you are inserting an apostrophe. Do not put it in just for good measure.

APOSTROPHES THAT SHORTEN WORDS

- <u>Contractions</u> combine <u>two</u> words into <u>one</u> with an apostrophe.
- <u>Abbreviations</u> are words in which letters have been <u>missed</u> <u>out</u>. <u>Apostrophes</u> <u>are</u> <u>used</u> <u>to</u> <u>show</u> <u>that</u> <u>one</u> <u>or</u> <u>more</u> <u>letters</u> <u>have</u> <u>been</u> <u>missed</u> <u>out</u>.

I'm = I am

Doesn't = Does not

Can't = Cannot

Won't = Will not

They're = They are

Would've = Would have

Examiner's Top Tip
Apostrophes are marks that help readers understand the intention of the writer. Use them to convey meaning as fully as you can.

USE AN APOSTROPHE WHEN WRITING THE TIME
- 'I will see Dave at 7 o'clock.' This is the short way of writing 'seven of the clock'.
- Missing numbers in dates can be suggested by an apostrophe:
  21st of September '99
  3rd of November '01

APOSTROPHES IN PLAYS
Playwrights such as Shakespeare shortened their words to allow their verse to remain in <u>iambic</u> <u>pentameter</u>. Shakespeare tried to divide his blank-verse lines into <u>10 syllables</u>, that is, <u>five</u> <u>feet</u> <u>of</u> <u>two</u> <u>syllables</u> <u>each</u>. Take this example from 'Romeo and Juliet', in which Romeo wants Juliet to exchange vows:
- Romeo: 'Th' exchange of thy love's faithful vow for mine.

APOSTROPHES IN DIALECT
Apostrophes are used a great deal by writers when they try to represent <u>local</u> <u>dialect</u>:
' 'ow's it goin' me ole mate?'
' 'awight, 'ow's it goin' yurself? I aint seen yu' in ages!'

- - - - - - - - - - - - - - - -

QUICK TEST

True or false?

1. Possessive pronouns can take apostrophes.

2. Apostrophes lengthen words.

3. Apostrophes can help show ownership.

4. If a person's name ends with an 's' you can put the apostrophe after it.

5. I ca'nt is correct.

6. Apostrophes of possession can help vary your sentences and can make them shorter.

6. True
5. False
4. True
3. True
2. False
1. False

THE MAIN TYPES OF SENTENCES

THERE ARE **FOUR** TYPES OF SENTENCE IN ENGLISH:
SIMPLE, COMPOUND, COMPLEX AND MINOR.

1. SIMPLE SENTENCES
Simple sentences must contain:
- a **subject** (the person or thing doing the action), e.g. Helen, the cat, I, they, the mad old professor
- a **verb** (the action), e.g. running, listens, slept, was alarmed

They can have other parts as well, such as:
- an **object** (the person of thing acted upon), e.g. Houses of Parliament, the field, him, her
- a **complement** (additional information about the subject), e.g. **Fadela** is a doctor
- **adverbials** (additional information about the verb), e.g. quickly, on Tuesday, at the house

When they form part of other sentences, simple sentences are usually referred to as '**clauses**'.

2. COMPOUND SENTENCES
join two or more sentences together. The two parts are joined by **coordinating conjunctions**, such as 'and', 'but' or 'or'.
e.g. Do you want to catch the bus **or** will you walk home?

3. COMPLEX SENTENCES
have two or more clauses joined by **subordinating conjunctions**, such as 'although', 'because' and 'if'. The main clause makes sense on its own. The subordinate clause does not make sense on its own. The subordinate clause follows the subordinating conjunction.
e.g. I didn't see you at the party **although** I looked everywhere.
If you read in this light, you'll hurt your eyes.
Note that the **subordinate clause** can occur at the beginning of the sentence as well as at the end.

4. MINOR SENTENCES
sentences usually consist of a single verb or verb phrase. They are often used in instructions.
e.g. Shut up!
Listen.
No smoking.

Examiner's Top Tip
Examiners are looking for a **variety** of sentences in your writing. Avoid too many sentences joined by coordinating conjunctions. Remember that short, sharp sentences can be very effective.

THE ANATOMY OF A SENTENCE

You probably know the names of the different parts of speech used in sentences, such as noun, pronoun, adjective, verb and adverb, conjunctions and prepositions. These can be single words, but they can also consist of short phrases.
e.g.

Old Alex walked slowly.
Adjective Noun Verb Adverb

Last Wednesday the early train was derailed unexpectedly.
Adverbial phrase Adjective Noun Verb phrase Adjective

It is important to remember that you can only tell what part of speech a word or phrase is when it is in a sentence. For instance:
London looks like a noun as it is the name of a place but in the sentence I caught the London bus it is an adjective.
Walk looks like a verb as it is an action but in the sentence They went for a walk it is a noun.

THE USE OF PRONOUNS

Pronouns are words that **stand in for nouns**, e.g. I, you, he, she, it, we, they, him, her, its, himself.
Pronouns are very useful but they can cause a number of problems. In a **compound sentence it makes sense not to repeat the noun**.
Aaron read the book and then he wrote a review.
is better than **Aaron read the book and then Aaron wrote a review.**

BUT you can overuse this technique and, if there is more than one character involved, it can be confusing. Can you understand the following sentence?
Patrick gave the CD to Joe but he was annoyed when he didn't tell him that he had recorded it.

The pronoun that causes most trouble is probably its.
Its is a **possessive pronoun** which causes problems because of its similarity to it's – the short form of it is, e.g. It's annoying when the dog loses its bone.
If you are having trouble deciding which version you should use, try expanding the short form to its longer form, e.g. **It is** annoying when the dog loses **it is** bone.
The first it's makes sense but the second one doesn't.

VARIETY WITHIN SENTENCES

As well as using all the different sentence types, you will impress examiners if you <u>vary</u> <u>the</u> <u>internal</u> <u>structure</u> <u>of</u> <u>your</u> <u>sentences</u>. Two ways of doing this involve:
• placing the most important information at the <u>beginning</u> of the sentence
• withholding important information until <u>the</u> <u>end</u> to create suspense.
For instance:

    Passing my driving test was probably one of the proudest moments of my life.

places emphasis on the passing of the test; whereas the sentence:

    One of the proudest moments of my life was probably passing my driving test.

uses exactly the same words but places the emphasis on how the speaker felt.

Even quite simple sentences can be rearranged according to what you are paying attention to.
The dog bit the man focuses on the dog.
The man was bitten by the dog focuses on the man.
The man was bitten eliminates the dog completely and
places more emphasis on the biting.

THE PASSIVE VOICE

The passive voice places emphasis on the **thing done rather than the person or thing performing an action**. It uses part of the verb 'to be' such as 'is' or 'was' plus a past participle such as 'heard' or 'taken', e.g.

    The voice of the turtle is heard in the land.
    Two pills are to be taken twice per day.
    The glass was broken.

The passive voice can be very useful for **avoiding responsibility**: The glass was broken is much more likely to get you off the hook than I broke the glass. It can also be used when the **person who performed an action is not known**: The wheel was discovered thousands of years ago.

Or it can be used when the **actor is not important** as in a scientific experiment: The measurements were taken at regular intervals.

But… Overuse of the passive should be avoided. Writing is **rather flat** if you don't know who is doing what. Passive sentences can sound **over formal** and they can be **confusing**: The enemy's throat was cut with a dagger is rather less exciting than I cut my enemy's throat with a dagger.

SENTENCES

Examiner's Top Tip
A recent survey showed that A* candidates used the most simple sentences and made good noun and verb choices.
C candidates often 'overloaded' sentences with too many adjectives.
D candidates tended to overuse compound sentences and used too many pronouns.

QUICK TEST

True or false?

1. A phrase can be a sentence.

2. Independent clauses can make sense on their own.

3. 'When you look into them' is a sentence.

4. The sentence, 'Write your name in block capitals' is a statement.

5. Varying your sentences can improve your expression.

5. True
4. False: it is a command or an instruction.
3. False
2. True
1. False

SPELLINGS AND WAYS TO LEARN THEM

METHODS OF LEARNING TRICKY SPELLINGS

1. The first piece of advice seems obvious, yet it is surprising how little it is taken – look up words in dictionaries and check their spellings. Dictionaries work on the alphabet principle for each word and finding words becomes easier with practice. Carry a small dictionary with you. Relying on teachers and others to spell words for you means that you will never really learn them. Aim to be an independent learner.

2. The Look–Say–Cover–Write–Check method is a successful one as long as you have spelled the word correctly in the first place. Learning words by repeating this process does work.

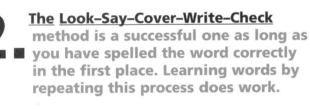

3. Try writing **a crazy but memorable sentence** using each letter of the word **(a mnemonic)**. Take for example, the word **believe**. **B**ig **e**lephants **l**ook **i**nside **e**lephantine **v**ases **e**verywhere. Only use this method for the few words that are the biggest bugbears for you, otherwise you will have too many strange phrases to remember.

4. Use the sound of words to help you spell them. Work your way through each syllable as you aim to spell the word. This works for many words and is always worth trying before using other methods.

5. For tricky plural endings follow the rules in 5, 6 and 7. If a noun ends with a 'y' and it has a letter such as 't', 'r' or 'n' before the y, you need to add 'ies' to the plural. **EXAMPLE** diar**y** – diaries, curr**y** – curries, compa**ny** – companies, ci**t**y – cities

6. If the **last letter before the 'y' is a vowel** (a, e, i, o, u) you have to add an '**s**' to make the plural. **EXAMPLE** b**oy** – boys, journ**ey** – journeys, key – keys, g**uy** – guys, monkey – monkeys

7. Words which end in '**fe**' such as knife take '**ves**' in plurals; similarly, words ending in '**f**' like **shelf** or **half** change to **shelves** and **halves** in plurals.

8. Use 'i' before 'e' except after 'c'. For example, **receive**.

Proof-read your work for words that you know you are likely to get wrong. Make a list of these words from a number of subjects and focus on learning them.

WORD FAMILIES

A good way of improving your spelling is to realise that words belong to families, so that, if you know the basic word, you will have a good idea about other similar words. For instance, the spelling of *criticism* is easier if you remember that it is related to *critic*. Here are some other useful word families.

<u>act</u>, actor, action, activity, react, reaction

<u>assist</u>, assistant, assistance

<u>balance</u>, imbalance, unbalanced

<u>bore</u>, boring, boredom

<u>call</u>, recall, calling

<u>claim</u>, reclaim, reclamation, disclaim

<u>child</u>, children, childhood, childlike, childish, childless

<u>cover</u>, discover, discovery, uncover

<u>critic</u>, criticism, criticise, critique

<u>electric</u>, electrical, electricity, electrician, electronic, electrocute

<u>examine</u>, examination, examiner, examinee

<u>fill</u>, fulfil, fulfilling, fulfilment

<u>give</u>, given, forgive, forgiveness

<u>govern</u>, governor, government,

<u>hand</u>, handler, handy, handicraft

<u>hero</u>, heroic, heroism

<u>joy</u>, joyful, enjoy, enjoyment

<u>light</u>, lightening, lightning, delighted, enlighten

<u>machine</u>, machinery, machinist

<u>medic</u>, medical, medication

<u>native</u>, nation, national, nativity

<u>nature</u>, natural, unnatural, denatured

<u>obey</u>, disobey, disobedient

<u>operate</u>, operator, cooperate, cooperation

<u>pack</u>, packet, package

<u>pain</u>, painkiller, painful, painless, painstaking

<u>pass</u>, passage, passenger

<u>press</u>, impress, depression, repress, express

<u>prison</u>, imprison, imprisonment

<u>prove</u>, approval, disapprove,

<u>public</u>, publication, publicity, publicise

<u>relate</u>, relative, relation

<u>shake</u>, shakily, shaken

<u>sign,</u> signatory, signature, signal, resign, resignation

<u>sum</u>, summary, summation, assume, assumption

<u>syllable</u>, monosyllable, monosyllabic, polysyllabic

<u>take</u>, mistake, mistaken, overtaken, overtaking, partaking

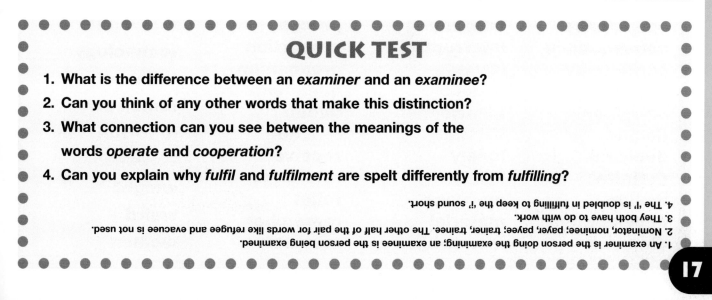

QUICK TEST

1. **What is the difference between an *examiner* and an *examinee*?**
2. **Can you think of any other words that make this distinction?**
3. **What connection can you see between the meanings of the words *operate* and *cooperation*?**
4. **Can you explain why *fulfil* and *fulfilment* are spelt differently from *fulfilling*?**

4. The 'l' is doubled in fulfilling to keep the 'i' sound short.
3. They both have to do with work.
2. Nominator, nominee; payer, payee; trainer, trainee. The other half of the pair for words like refugee and evacuee is not used.
1. An examiner is the person doing the examining; an examinee is the person being examined.

A CHECKLIST OF WORDS OFTEN MISSPELLED

COMMONLY MISSPELLED WORDS

A–F

accommodation
actually
alcohol
although
analyse
analysis
argument
assessment
atmosphere
audible
audience
autumn
beautiful
beginning
believe
beneath
buried
business
caught
chocolate
climb
column
concentration
conclusion
conscience
consequence
continuous
creation
daughter
decide
decision
definite
design
development
diamond
diary
disappear
disappoint
embarrass
energy
engagement
enquire
environment
evaluation
evidence
explanation
February
fierce
forty
fulfil
furthermore

G–P

guard
happened
health
height
imaginary
improvise
industrial
interesting
interrupt
issue
jealous
knowledge
listening
lonely
lovely
marriage
material
meanwhile
miscellaneous
mischief
modern
moreover
murmur
necessary
nervous
original
outrageous

P–R

parallel
participation
pattern
peaceful
people
performance
permanent
persuade
persuasion
physical
possession
potential
preparation
prioritise
process
proportion
proposition
questionnaire
queue
reaction
receive
reference
relief
remember
research
resources

S–W

safety
Saturday
secondary
separate
sequence
shoulder
sincerely
skilful
soldier
stomach
straight
strategy
strength
success
surely
surprise
survey
technique
technology
texture
tomorrow
unfortunately
Wednesday
weight
weird
women

COMMON HOMOPHONES AND CONFUSIONS

a lot, allot
never alot as a single word

advise, advice
to advise, to give advice

affect, effect
to influence, a result

allowed, aloud
permitted, out loud

are, our
part of the verb to be, belonging to us

bean, been
as in baked bean, part of the verb to be

beech, beach
tree, seashore

blue, blew
colour, air moved

board, bored
wood or group of managers, uninterested

bought, brought
purchased, carried

break, brake
damage, slow down

by, buy, bye
next to or responsible for, purchase, farewell

cell, sell
enclosed space, dispose of for money

cent, scent, sent
coin, smell, dispatched

cereal, serial
type of grain, a story in parts

choose, chose
decide – present tense, decide – past tense

cloth, clothe
material, to dress

conscience, conscious
sense of right or wrong, aware

course, coarse
route or direction, rough

dear, deer
beloved or expensive, mammal

fate, fete
inevitable force, celebration

flour, flower
bread ingredient, part of plant

grate, great
scrape, very large

hair, hare
on head, animal

herd, heard
group, listened to

here, hear
this place, listen

him, hymn
that man, religious song

hole, whole
pit, complete

hour, our
time, belonging to us

it's, its
it is, belonging to it

key, quay
lock opener, boat dock

knight, night
wears armour, darkness

knot, not
rope tie or nautical speed, negative

know, no
be aware, negative

made, maid
built or done, female worker

main, mane
important or the sea, lion's hair

meet, meat
come together, animal flesh

might, mite
possibly or strength, small insect or small amount

morning, mourning
early part of day, marking a death

new, knew
recent, was aware

pane, pain
part of window, hurt

peace, piece
quiet, segment or part

place, plaice
location, fish

plane, plain
flat (in maths) or short for airplane, not beautiful or large expanse of flat land

practise, practice
to practise, a practice

quiet, quite
not loud, fairly

read, reed
activity with text, sort of grass

rein, rain, reign
horse equipment, water, royal rule

right, write
correct, use pen

rode, road, rowed
used vehicle, carriageway, used oars

scene, seen
part of play, looked at

see, sea
look, body of water

sew, so, sow
use needle and thread, intensifier, scatter seed

sites, sights
places, things seen or aiming device

source, sauce
origin, food supplement

stair, stare
steps, look hard

steel, steal
metal, take

sum, some
total, a few

sun, son
thing in sky, male descendant

tail, tale
part of animal, story

their, they're, there
belonging to them, they are, that place

too, two, to
in addition, 2, in the direction of

vain, vein
self admiring, blood vessel

waist, waste
below stomach, not used

week, weak
seven days, without strength

where, were, wear
which place, used to be, clothe

you, yew, ewe
person, tree, female sheep

you're, your
you are, belonging to you

SYNONYMS

These are words that mean the same.

EXAMPLES

beautiful = pretty, nice, fine, good-looking, elegant, lovely, fair

display = show, exhibit, exhibition, spread, open, expose, demonstration, layout

Examiner's Top Tip
English is a notoriously difficult language to spell but with effort you can overcome most obvious misspellings. There are people who can spell well and those who do not make serious effort! Why not go through the lists here and try some of the exercises suggested on the previous pages? The main one is: Look–Say–Cover–Write–Check.

PUTTING YOUR IDEAS IN THE RIGHT ORDER

WORDS THAT HELP PUT YOUR IDEAS IN ORDER
· firstly, then, so far, secondly, in the end, next, eventually, subsequently, at last, at length, afterwards

WORDS FOR EXCEPTIONS
· only, if, unless, except (for), save for

Examiner's Top Tip
The skilful use of connectives can help you vary your sentence structure and improve your style.

MAKING POINTS AND GIVING EXAMPLES

WORDS TO USE TO ARGUE AND MAKE POINTS
• consequently, thus, so, as a result, because, as, hence, therefore, since, until, whenever, accordingly, as long as

WORDS TO HELP YOU GIVE EXAMPLES
• for example, for instance, such as, take the case of, thus, as (evidence), to show that, as revealed by

WORDS FOR EXTRA POINTS OR IDEAS
• and, too, what is more, also, furthermore, and then, again, moreover, as well as, in addition

WORDS WHICH HELP YOU EMPHASISE POINTS
• above all, in particular, notably, specifically, indeed, more important, especially, significant(ly), in fact

PARAGRAPHING

Paragraphs are necessary to give the readers a rest and help them to follow the writer's meaning.
• Paragraphs are groups of sentences connected by the same topic. Each paragraph carries a main idea.
• The main sentence of a paragraph is often found at the beginning and it is called a topic sentence. For example: Successful students plan their revision in each subject. They plan how much time they have available and then try to cover a number of areas in each subject.
• Any paragraphs following the first paragraph will need to begin on a new line, indented 2 cm from the page margin. In business correspondence or word-processed work there is no need to indent new paragraphs.
• You can link your paragraphs together skilfully by using the connecting words found in the boxes on these pages.

BEING PERSUASIVE AND ANALYTICAL

WORDS TO PERSUADE
• of course, naturally, obviously, clearly, certainly, surely, evidently

WORDS TO HELP YOU SHOW AN OPINION OR ANALYSE
• it would seem, to suggest, one might conclude/propose/deduce/infer/imply/say/consider

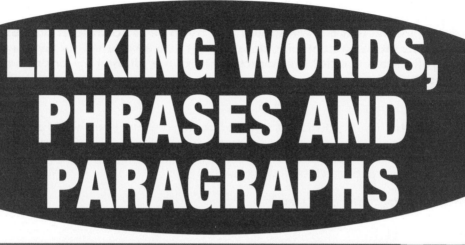

LINKING WORDS, PHRASES AND PARAGRAPHS

COMPARING AND CONTRASTING

WORDS TO MAKE A CONTRAST OR SHOW WHAT IS DIFFERENT
• *but, nevertheless, alternatively, despite this, on the contrary, however, yet, the opposite, instead, whereas, to turn to, although, still, on the other hand*

WORDS TO COMPARE THINGS IN YOUR WRITING OR SHOW WHAT IS THE SAME
• *equally, in the same way, as with, likewise, similarly, compared with, an equivalent*

ESSAY ENDINGS

WORDS TO SUM UP OR END WITH
• in brief, in summary, throughout, in all, on the whole, to sum up, overall, finally, to conclude, to recap, in the end

Examiner's Top Tip
Use appropriate and varied connective words in your essays to signpost your arguments.

QUICK TEST

1. Why use paragraphs?

2. Identify two words that can help you compare pieces of writing.

3. What is the difference between comparing and contrasting?

4. Give two words that help emphasise points in writing.

5. What do these words help you to do: 'furthermore' and 'moreover'.

5. They help you make extra points or ideas.
4. Indeed, in particular, above all, notably, specifically, more importantly, especially, significantly(ly), in fact (any of these)
3. To 'compare' is to look for similarities and to 'contrast' is to look for differences.
2. In the same way, similarly, equally, as with, likewise, compared with, an equivalent (any of these)
1. Paragraphs help readers follow your ideas. They also break up too much text which readers can find off-putting.

IMPROVE YOUR STYLE

Examiner's Top Tip
A clear, fluent, written style is something that you are going to have to work at. Examine the style of the writers you are studying and think about phrases, words and punctuation that could work for you.

CONTROL

Teachers and examiners are looking for <u>control</u> in your writing. This means an awareness of the effect that different writing techniques can have and <u>deliberate</u> use of them.

VOCABULARY AND CHOICE OF WORDS

The first thing you need to think about is <u>the</u> <u>words</u> <u>you</u> <u>choose</u>. This needs to be appropriate for the text but you should also try to be as accurate as possible. When one of your characters gets into an automobile, does she get into a battered old Ford, a people carrier or an oversized all terrain vehicle? Do characters say things all the time or do they mutter, mumble or shout?

VARYING SENTENCE AND PARAGRAPHS

You already know about using different types of sentences, but you should also think about the <u>rhythm</u> <u>of</u> <u>your</u> <u>writing</u>. Large stretches of long sentences can create a sense of <u>continuity</u> and <u>flow</u>, but they can become monotonous. <u>Try</u> <u>short</u> <u>sentences</u> <u>for</u> <u>emphasis</u>. Even more emphatic than the short sentence is the short paragraph.

A single sentence paragraph really stands out.

BUILDING TENSION

Another use for short sentences is in building <u>tension</u> and <u>atmosphere</u>. For instance, in a piece of genre fiction, such as horror writing, you can build up tension by using short, snappy sentences that <u>make</u> <u>the</u> <u>reader</u> <u>pause</u> <u>over</u> <u>each</u> <u>detail</u>.

'I ran. Ran for all I was worth! Sometimes I stumbled over tree roots. Branches slashed my face. Something was rapidly hunting me down. Twigs and branches snapped in the desperate rushing behind me. A savage, wolf-like howl tore the air. Something clasped my leg! "God help me!" I screamed, as I gasped for breath.'

VARYING SENTENCE STRUCTURES

The first part of a sentence tends to contain <u>the</u> <u>subject</u>. In the middle of a piece of writing this is often <u>known</u> information – the new information comes at the end. From time to time you can vary this order. Compare the impact of:

As I put the car into gear the engine went 'thunk'.

with   'Thunk,' went the engine as I put the car into gear.

You also have a great deal of choice when it comes to the placing of <u>adverbial</u> <u>phrases</u>. These tell you about things like time, mood and manner. For instance:

With deliberate slowness, Dr Shrike marked out the area he was going to cut.

Dr Shrike, with deliberate slowness, marked out the area he was going to cut.

Dr Shrike marked out the area he was going to cut with deliberate slowness.

DESCRIPTIVE WRITING

The power of descriptive writing comes in the <u>accurate</u> <u>choice</u> <u>of</u> <u>nouns</u> <u>and</u> <u>verbs</u>. Adjectives and adverbs can help to pin down what you say even more accurately. Always make sure that your adjectives or adverbs are <u>doing</u> <u>some</u> <u>work</u>. For instance, 'he walked slowly' could be conveyed with the single verb 'he strolled'. A 'gnarled oak' will create a much clearer picture in your readers' minds than 'a big twisted tree'. Finally, remember to appeal to <u>all five senses</u> in descriptive writing.

SOME PITFALLS TO AVOID

<u>Do</u> <u>not</u> <u>confuse</u> <u>big</u> <u>words</u> <u>with</u> <u>a</u> <u>sophisticated</u> <u>style</u>. Remember that you want to give your readers as clear a picture as possible.

<u>Do</u> <u>not</u> <u>overdo</u> <u>any</u> <u>one</u> <u>effect</u>. If all your sentences have an unusual structure, people will find it distracting.

<u>Use</u> <u>figurative</u> <u>language</u> <u>sparingly</u>. One well chosen simile or metaphor will stand out like a rose in a desert.

CLARITY AND BREVITY

Keep what you write brief, simple and clear. Avoid long-winded, pompous sentences.

- 'I remained in my abode and passed the time watching uninteresting programmes while looking at the little box in the corner.'

This is tedious. Try this instead:

- 'I stayed at home watching boring programmes on TV.'

UNNECESSARY REPETITION

Avoid using tautologies; that is repeating yourself unnecessarily. Also try to avoid reinforcing words with words that would be better left out. Your writing will have more impact without them. Tautologies to avoid:

- final end
- sad misfortune
- puzzling mystery

Word-reinforcement to avoid

- totally wrong
- absolutely fantastic
- seriously consider

OVERWORKED INFORMAL WORDS

Avoid overworked words because they can be boring and repetitive.

Examples:

- got, get, nice, good, totally, a lot of, kind of

These are too casual to be used as formal, standard English.

CIRCUMLOCUTIONS

Circumlocutions are roundabout ways of saying things. Again, stick to simple words or expressions, as these are more effective.

- few in number = few
- in a majority of cases = usually
- in less than no time = quickly
- in the event that = if
- on the grounds that = because
- owing to the fact that = because
- prior to = before
- with the exception of = except

HOW TO IMPROVE YOUR EXPRESSION

CLICHÉS

Clichés are tired expressions and imagery that have lost any impact because of overuse. There are, of course, a host of such worn-out phrases often reached for by tired minds. Avoid the following:

- like the plague
- like two ships that pass in the night
- food for thought
- leaves much to be desired
- leave no stone unturned
- shoot oneself in the foot
- we will deliver (that is, doing something – a favourite cliché of politicians!)

WRITING EFFECTIVE SENTENCES

For a stylish, effective sentence the importance of each part is as follows:

- the beginning is the second-most important part
- the middle is least important
- the end is the most important.

Take, for example, this line from Shakespeare's *Twelfth Night* given to Malvolio: 'Some are born great, some achieve greatness and some have greatness thrust upon 'em.'

QUICK TEST

1. **Reduce these phrases to one word:**

   a) **Due to the fact that**

   b) **Pink in colour**

   c) **In this day and age**

2. **What is the danger of overdoing description?**

3. **Identify a cliché and explain why you should try to avoid clichés in writing.**

Examiner's Top Tip
Try to improve your expression as you develop the habit of proof-reading your work. The Russian writer Chekhov said, 'Rewrite everything five times!'

3. 'Shot in the foot'. The image has no impact and will simply pass readers by, or worse, bore them. There are numerous examples.
2. The readers could lose sight of your meaning.
1. a) because b) pink c) now

SPEAKING AND LISTENING

HOW YOU WILL BE GRADED

- Can you speak with purpose in a structured way? You need to signpost your points when you speak so that others can follow what you are saying and do not get bored.

- Are you able to speak with fluency and confidence on your chosen topic with minimal notes? Do not make the mistake of reading your notes. Someone with their head stuck in their notes, losing their place and starting their points again is not very impressive.

- Do you vary the sound of your voice to interest your audience? Do you use eye contact and other body language to interest your listener? Sixty per cent of any communication is non-verbal! This means that you use body language such as posture, hand gestures and eye contact as well as varying the tone and pitch of your voice when you speak. This is how people understand what you mean. All these things are converted into punctuation when you write down what you are saying. Writing is therefore a very poor substitute for speaking. It is difficult to get exactly what you mean across to someone when you write because you are not usually there to animate your words.

- Can you adapt the register of your speech to the task and your audience? You would hardly speak to your head-teacher using the same tone of voice as you would to your best friends. You need to be conscious of how people adapt their speech to those they talk to.

- Are you able to use standard English with confidence in a range of situations? How fluent is your standard English? Do you drop into your local dialect without realising that you are doing so? You need to be more conscious of when you use dialect as well as why, where and to whom you would use standard English. If you were answering a phone in an office you would not use local dialect. It all comes down to being polite, especially with people we do not know. They need to understand us.

- Can you initiate speech, sustain a point of view or manage the contributions of others? If so, you would make a great host of a discussion panel.

- Can you listen with sensitivity and respond accordingly? Are you able to carry forward and further the arguments of others and follow a complex conversation?

CAN YOU:
- skilfully involve listeners?
- speak with irony?
- show flair or make thought-provoking contributions?
- show that you have a wide vocabulary?
- use rhetorical techniques?

Examiner's Top Tip
Take turns in speaking and show that you listen!

WHAT YOU WILL DO

<u>You</u> <u>will</u> <u>need</u> <u>to</u> <u>do</u> <u>a</u> <u>minimum</u> <u>of</u> <u>three</u> <u>orals</u>, at least one of each of the following:

SINGLE ORAL
Pick a subject that only you could talk about. Choose something that you know really well and would enjoy talking about.

PAIRED ORAL
This is a good one in which to analyse junk mail, a poem or any story. Maybe you would like to look at an issue in the news and explore and analyse it?

GROUP
<u>This</u> <u>is</u> <u>excellent</u> <u>for</u> <u>debates</u> <u>and</u> <u>anything</u> <u>to</u> <u>do</u> <u>with</u> <u>teamwork</u>.

- <u>You</u> <u>can</u> <u>do</u> <u>more</u> <u>than</u> <u>three</u> <u>orals</u> <u>but</u> <u>only</u> <u>your</u> <u>best</u> <u>grades</u> <u>in</u> <u>each</u> <u>set</u> <u>of</u> <u>criteria</u> <u>will</u> <u>be</u> <u>counted</u>; so do as many as you can! The orals can be done in any order so long as you have covered the objectives on the right.
- <u>It</u> <u>is</u> <u>advisable</u> <u>to</u> <u>keep</u> <u>a</u> <u>written</u> <u>record</u> <u>of</u> <u>your</u> <u>oral</u>. If you do, then you need to give some details of what the oral was about. Then explain how the oral went.
- You should say what went well and identify areas for <u>improvement</u>.
- Some activities will also cover more than one set of criteria so it is therefore acceptable (sometimes) to cover the same criteria twice.

These are the three main marking criteria for the orals that you have to do:

EXPLAIN, DESCRIBE OR NARRATE
This is good for autobiographical stories, work placements, explaining a story that you have written, your main hobby, etc.

EXPLORE, ANALYSE OR IMAGINE
This can be very wide-ranging. Good things to talk about here are persuasive techniques in junk mail and the imagery and themes of poems, stories, etc.

DISCUSS, ARGUE OR PERSUADE
Great for debates, burning issues that concern your life, topics in the news, etc. Maybe something could be debated out of a poem, story or novel that you have read in class. For instance, is Tess of the D'Urbervilles really 'A Pure Woman' as the subtitle of Thomas Hardy's book suggests?

Examiner's Top Tip
Try to relax when you do your orals. Remember that this is a chance to boost your grades. Your teacher knows you and will want to give you the highest grade that you deserve.

STANDARD ENGLISH

- This is formal, the English you should use with people that you do not know. The aim is to be clearly understood by anyone. Teachers usually use it! In other words, do not use 'Me and Danielle ain't saw each other for ages' when 'Danielle and I have not seen each other for ages' is called for.
- In formal situations avoid your <u>local dialect</u>. This should be used for talking to your family, friends or neighbours. <u>There is nothing wrong with dialect. It is the correct, friendly language to use in informal situations</u>. Use it when you talk to your friends and family. It is alright then to say, "'ere, mate, could ya pass us the bu''er.'

QUICK TEST

1. How many orals do you need to take and what must each of them be?

2. What is standard English and when should you use it?

3. Why would you use body language?

4. With whom would you use dialect?

5. Why is it important to listen?

5. Conversations need listeners too. You can make better points.
4. With family and friends
3. It helps people understand you and makes your speech more interesting.
2. Formal English: use it in formal situations.
1. Three: single, paired and group

LIBRARIAN, MID-KENT COLLEGE OF HIGHER & FURTHER EDUCATION OAKWOOD PARK, TONBRIDGE ROAD MAIDSTONE, KENT ME16 8AQ

SPEAKING AND LISTENING: PREPARING AND GIVING A TALK

By choosing/buying this book you have shown that you have initiative and that you are an independent learner. Why not try this:
* *With a partner, talk about how a leaflet informs, explains or describes.*
* *Show how some leaflets persuade, discuss and argue.*
* *Save and use any interesting junk mail that arrives through your letterbox. In particular, look for letters written by charities and anything with interesting fonts and pictures. Other good sources for excellent leaflets are public libraries, and doctors' and dentists' surgeries.*
* *See the checklists on 'Language' and 'Layout' of the media section of this book on pages 40–41 to help you prepare for this talk.*

PREPARING YOUR TALK

1. THE TOPIC
* If you are allowed, choose a topic that interests you. It could be your work placement or perhaps a hobby or a mania.
* Your talk will be to:

  * explain, describe or narrate * explore, analyse or imagine * discuss, argue or persuade

* Think of a suitable title for your talk. This will help you focus on your topic.
* Research your topic. Talk to experts; do some research on the Internet; look in encyclopedias; check out your library; write to agencies, companies or embassies.
* Gather resources to help you with your details, points and arguments. Find and prepare any props that you need now. They will be useful for focusing and keeping your audience's attention on what you are saying.

2. THE STRUCTURE
* Think about the structure of your talk: introduction, body and conclusion.
* Summarise the talk in a few paragraphs. Keep them brief.
* Brainstorm your talk into a flow chart.

3. THE PROMPTS
* Cut up several square pieces of card just smaller than a postcard.
* Write down your main ideas in words or phrases to remind you of what you intend to say. Resist the temptation to write too much. Keep to brief points because you will use them as prompts.
* Write the words or phrases twice the size of your normal writing. This is for your own self-assurance as you speak. If you forget your next point, just glance at your card. Turn over the cards as you speak.
* Spread out your cards on a table and pick them up in the correct order. Number the cards in the right order. The structure of your talk will then be clear for you as well as your audience.

4. PRACTICE
* Practise your talk to get the structure and any specialised or unusual vocabulary clear in your mind.
* Think about the necessity of using standard English and consider any places in your talk where you might pause and welcome questions. Questions could act as ice-breakers and help you relax. You will also be able to gauge the impact of the early parts of your talk.
* Practise any unusual or specialised vocabulary so that you appear confident and do not stumble over topic-specific terms.
* Remember to get props or handouts ready if you need them and pack them in your bag the night before you go to school.

Examiner's Top Tip
Remember to show that you are also a good listener. Do not talk over people. Take turns in speech. However, you do need to say something in group talks, otherwise it will be impossible for your teacher to assess you fully.

GIVING THE TALK

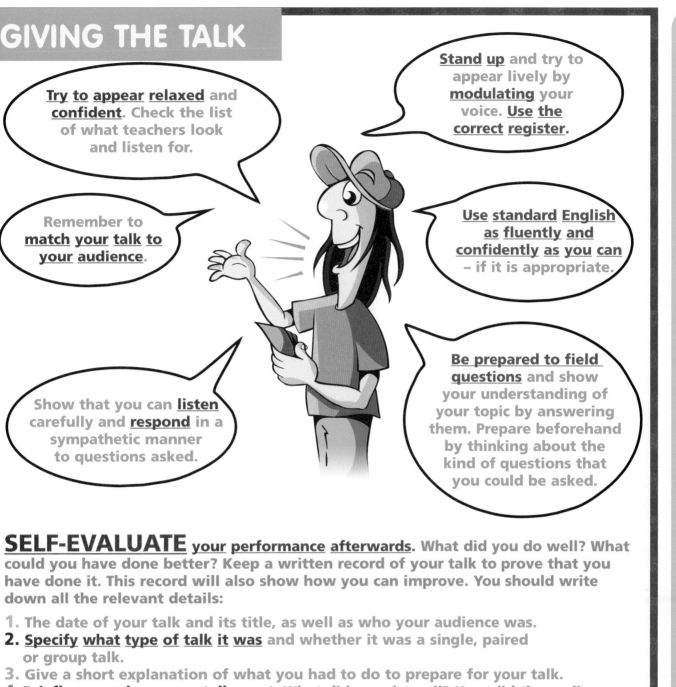

Try to appear relaxed and **confident**. Check the list of what teachers look and listen for.

Stand up and try to appear lively by **modulating** your voice. **Use the correct register**.

Remember to match your talk to your audience.

Use standard English as fluently and confidently as you can – if it is appropriate.

Show that you can **listen** carefully and **respond** in a sympathetic manner to questions asked.

Be prepared to field questions and show your understanding of your topic by answering them. Prepare beforehand by thinking about the kind of questions that you could be asked.

SELF-EVALUATE your performance afterwards.

What did you do well? What could you have done better? Keep a written record of your talk to prove that you have done it. This record will also show how you can improve. You should write down all the relevant details:

1. The date of your talk and its title, as well as who your audience was.
2. **Specify what type of talk it was** and whether it was a single, paired or group talk.
3. Give a short explanation of what you had to do to prepare for your talk.
4. **Briefly assess how your talk went.** What did you do well? How did the audience respond to your talk?
5. Complete your record by **identifying two or three areas for improvement**. You should get these from your teacher's feedback. However, you may also be aware of these areas yourself once you have given your talk.

QUICK TEST

1. Why is it important to plan your talk?
2. Towards the end of your talk what might you do to involve your audience?
3. What is standard English?

Examiner's Top Tip
Do not just read your notes aloud. You are not being tested on your ability to read. A major aim is to talk in the most fluent and confident manner that you can.

3. This is formal English in which you pronounce all your words correctly and avoid using local dialect.
2. Ask questions or show them props.
1. It helps give a more coherent structure and more detail.

Punctuation and Sentences

1. Try to sum up in a sentence why you need to punctuate your writing.

....

2. Identify five instances where you would need a capital letter.

....

3. Correct the following sentences by putting in capital letters where they are necessary:
   jemma read *Great Expectations* for her english course-work. she had never read charles dickens before; she may read another one of his novels before easter.

....

4. Identify four of the five punctuation marks that can complete a sentence.

....

5. Explain one of the uses that semi-colons can serve.

....

6. What is a rhetorical question?

....

7. Identify one use for colons.

....

8. Give three of the four rules of direct speech.

....

9. What are the two main purposes of apostrophes?

....

10. Where does the apostrophe need to go with plural nouns that do not need an 's' to make them plurals?

....

11. Identify three of the four types of sentences.

....

12. Point out the main and dependent clauses of this sentence:
    I will go to see the new movie at the cinema as soon I have done the washing up.

....

Spelling and Expression

13. Point out two methods of learning tricky spellings.

....

14. What is before 'e' except after 'c'?

....

15. Why do the following plurals end in 'ies'?
    twenties, lorries, cities, injuries and berries.

....

16. Why do the following plurals end in 's'?
    journeys, trolleys, donkeys, chimneys, toys.

....

17. What do 'here', 'there' and 'where' have in common?

....

18. Correct the following spellings:
    begginning, apperance, intrested, grammer, tonge, definately, neccesity, rythm, sentance.

....

19. What are synonyms?

....

20. Why are homophones confusing?

....

21. What are connectives?

....

22. What is the purpose of connectives in writing?

....

23. Why is it necessary to use paragraphs?

....

24. What is a topic sentence?

....

25. Briefly explain what 'control' means in writing.

....

26. Reduce this circumlocution to one word: 'on the grounds that'.

....

Speaking and Listening

27. How many orals do you need to do?

....

28. What must each of them be?

....

29. What is dialect?

....

30. Identify three dialects that can be found in Britain.

....

31. Briefly explain what is meant by standard English.

....

32. When, where and to whom would you use standard English and your local dialect?

....

33. Identify two things that you should keep a note of once you have given your oral in class.

....

34. Briefly explain what is meant by 'body language'.

....

35. What is 'register' in speech?

....

36. Explain what is meant by 'irony'.

....

37. Why is it important to listen?

....

38. What does the word 'analyse' mean?

....

39. What kinds of assignments are suitable for discussing, arguing and persuading?

....

40. Why is it important that you do not write out long passages for your talk?

....

41. What is meant by 'structure' in a talk?

....

42. Why is it important to self-assess after your talk?

....

How did you do?

1–10	correct	.start again
11–20	correct	.getting there
21–32	correct	.good work
33–42	correct	.excellent

ORIGINAL WRITING (EN3)

WHAT YOU ARE EXPECTED TO DO

Your task is to produce a piece of writing that either <u>explores</u>, <u>imagines</u> or <u>entertains</u> for one or more specific audiences. (Your piece could include all the criteria.)

- In this section you will be assessed on the **quality** of your writing and not on the texts that you have read. There is a wide range of possibilities of what you may write about because there are no restrictions on <u>form,</u> <u>content</u> or <u>genre</u>.

- The exam boards do not usually specify any particular **length** for your work in terms of words or pages; however most of them think that around <u>1000</u> <u>words</u> should be long enough for an accurate assessment of your work to be made. For example, if you submitted a group of poems and wrote a brief account of their composition that would be fine; but long, wordy, unfocused projects are not wanted. What is most important is that the written piece has <u>clear</u> <u>aims</u>, a <u>specific</u> <u>purpose</u>, a <u>particular</u> <u>audience</u> and that it is <u>effectively</u> <u>written</u>. If your work is <u>convincing</u> and <u>concise</u> then the examiner must give it a high mark.

- Teachers are conscious of the **limited** **time** available to cover both course-work and exam elements of the GSCE. Sometimes they try to cover two or more parts of your coursework using the same topic. For instance, it is not unusual for a media assignment on the comparison of two soaps to extend to a group-oral presentation on a new soap opera. Each member of the group might then go on to produce a piece of original writing by composing a short episode of their soap opera. <u>Media</u> <u>assignments</u> can lend themselves to such creative results.

Examiner's Top Tip
When you produce drafts of your work, leave an empty line between each line of text. This will allow you to proof-read more easily, and you can always pencil corrections in the blank lines.

INTERNET

Web sites for examples of excellent stories:
http://164.106.182.10:276/serfweb/phillips/
common/webdocs/ClassicStorylinks.hmtl

http://mbhs.bergtraum.k12.ny.us/cybereng/shorts/

http://www.short-stories.co.uk/

• **If you do not like writing stories, you could write an extra chapter for a novel or a scene from a play that you have read. You could, perhaps, write a few diary entries from any major character that impressed you from the texts in your coursework. However, check first that diaries fill the grading criteria for pieces of coursework for your GCSE in Literature.**

WHAT YOU CAN WRITE ABOUT

Here are a few suggested tasks that you could choose from for a fictional piece of writing of 1000 words or so for a story; obviously you would use fewer words for poetry.

Produce a few poems or a long poem such as a ballad to retell an interesting story from the news. Read a few ballads such as *The Lady of Shallot* or *The Ballad of Frankie and Johnny* to get an idea of the form and the effect you can gain from repeating lines and using rhyme in quatrains (four-line stanzas). Notice the rhythm and tone of ballads – in other words, how they sound when read aloud. Could you choose words which would give your poem an appropriate rhythm and tone?

Devise a soap opera and explain the rationale behind its setting, characters, plots and envisaged audience.

Write an extra chapter for a novel.

Write a short horror story with a 'twist in the tale'.

Write an episode or a few detailed scenes for a soap opera.

Write detailed descriptions of people and places with the aim of entertaining and amusing your audience.

Write a one-act play.

Keep an imaginary diary.

HOW YOU WILL BE GRADED

To achieve a good grade from C to A* you will need to:

- write in the appropriate manner for the genre and purpose of your story

- use a varied range of sentences and vocabulary to keep your audience's interest

- keep punctuation accurate and produce logical paragraphs to make your meaning clear

- develop characters and settings within your narrative

- use literary devices such as similes and metaphors effectively

- show assured control in your writing with a wide range of expression to achieve effects

- show an awareness of tone in words and sentences

- be almost faultless in punctuation and spelling

- write with flair and originality

- show that you can be elaborate or concise.

INTERNET

If you would like to read an excellent story with an ingenious ending read **Liam O'Flaherty's** *The Sniper*.

You can find it at:
http://mbhs.bergraum.k12.ny.us/ cybereng/shorts/sniper.hmtl

This story has a very short time-frame: its action takes place over a few hours. You could do the same in your story by writing about a single incident or an episode that lasts for only a few hours.

Here are a few titles to get you going if you are stuck for ideas:
**'My Last Day on Earth'
'Strange Meeting'
'Emergency on Alpha Minor'
'Danger in Venice'
'The Visitors'
'A Day in my Life as a Dog'**

Examiner's Top Tip
Remember that this work is also a dry run for the exam essay. Each piece of writing will need a plan, no matter how brief.

HOW TO WRITE AND PLAN A STORY

PLANNING

Brainstorm or do a spidergram of your ideas on a blank sheet of paper. Sometimes stories can come from *a character*; sometimes they can come from *a specific situation* such as a shipwreck or a sudden discovery. Once you have a few ideas, try to think of a *title* because this may help you focus on the *plot* and *characterisation* of your story.

The plot is the plan or outline of your story.
What will be the *climax* of your plot when your story reaches a crisis? What will be the result of the *climax*? From whose *point of view* is the story going to be told? Decide if the style of narration is to be in the *first* or *third person*. *A first-person narrator tells the story from within the story; a third-person narrator stands outside the story.* How much will your narrator know and see? Will the third-person narrator be able to know everything that the characters are thinking? These are matters of *perspective. Will the narrator be biased or objective in their viewpoint*?

CHARACTERS

You will need a *main character* and *two or three* other important characters. You could include some minor ones, too. Create a brief *profile* for each character, as this will enable you to be realistic in your portrayal of them. *Have a checklist for each one,* for example, their age, appearance, habits, job, traits, ambitions, hobbies, likes and dislikes, motivation, etc.

SETTING

Where is the story going to be *set*? *Will it be set at home or abroad*? Is the story going to be set in the *present, future or past*? Will your story be drawn from everyday life? Perhaps you would prefer a fairy-tale setting drawn from your imagination? How are you going to describe the setting? Will you suggest the *setting* as you write with minor details or will you be more elaborate in the details that you give to describe the setting? If necessary do a little research to make your setting *convincing*.

GENRE

Choose a *genre* for your story. Is your story going to be an adventure, detective, love, science-fiction or comedy story? Can you be even more specific within your *genre* by going for a sub-division within it (for instance, *comedy-romance*)?

STRUCTURE

Ensure that you have a clear beginning, middle and end in your story. You need to bait your story with a good 'hook' at the beginning to make your readers read on. Perhaps you could begin in the middle of an exciting incident; you could use some unusual description or maybe start from an unusual perspective to intrigue the reader. Look at examples in stories you read.

WILL THERE BE A TWIST IN THE TALE?

If your story involves suspense try to include '<u>a twist in the tale</u>', or perhaps give a <u>moral</u> to your story.

USE OF TIME

How are you going to tell your story? Will you tell your story in a <u>linear</u> (straightforward) way or through flashbacks? The <u>plots</u> of most stories, novels and plays are written in a <u>linear</u> manner. Their plots and characters move forward naturally in time. In contrast, a novel such as 'Wuthering Heights' (1847) by Emily Brontë moves forwards and backwards in time as various first-person narrators relate significant events in the novel.

PERSONAL WRITING: FICTION AND THE IMAGINATION (EN3)

QUICK TEST

1. How is a first-person narrative told?
2. What does the term 'genre' mean?
3. What do you need at the beginning of a story to keep your readers interested in reading further?
4. What does it mean to be elaborate?
5. How can you make your characters believable?

Examiner's Top Tip
Remember that the last part of your sentence usually carries most impact so recast your sentences to maximise your impact, in order to give a powerful account of something imagined.

Examiner's Top Tip
Try to use a few literary devices such as similes, metaphors and alliteration in your writing to create effects.

1. By a character in the story, using 'I'.
2. A kind of writing, for example, detective stories, romance, science-fiction, etc.
3. An interesting 'hook' which will seize the attention of an audience
4. It means going into detail or extensive description.
5. Build up a profile for them; try to give them realistic speech.

PERSONAL WRITING: NON-FICTION

This means writing to: describe, explain, inform, instruct, entertain, report, review, persuade, witness, compare/contrast, request, complain and express feelings. A piece of writing like this could be submitted as coursework. You will definitely be asked to produce more pieces of writing like this in your exam.

WHAT YOU CAN WRITE ABOUT

an autobiographical piece about, say, a memorable trip or holiday that you made with your family; look at magazines which have 'A Day in the Life of Someone'. In some descriptive detail write about a day in your life for a young person's magazine. Think about your audience as you write your piece. Only you can write about your life so write it as well as you can!

a topic that interests you; explain the issue and give your view of it.

an interesting picture from a newspaper or a magazine; write about it in as much detail as you can.

THIS COULD BE:

a piece of writing in which you give your view on any subject, for example animal experimentation.

a discursive (digressive) essay about two sides of a topical issue in the news.

HOW YOU WILL BE GRADED

Examiner's Top Tip
Always consider the purpose, message, audience and the best form for your writing.

To achieve grades C to A* you will need to:
- research your chosen topic carefully
- show that your writing is organised and appropriate for your topic
- interest your readers and sustain points
- use an appropriate range of punctuation to make your meaning clear
- be as interesting and original as you can
- use your own words
- give a powerful account of a real experience
- show both elaboration and conciseness in your writing
- use appropriate registers; that is, match your tone and language to your audience
- use wide-ranging vocabulary in which syntax, spelling and punctuation is almost faultless
- consciously shape and craft language to achieve sophisticated effects
- use standard written forms in a convincing manner
- produce a well-organised and compelling piece of work.

When grading your work, examiners will take into account that you had more time to prepare and present your coursework and will understand that you have limited time in exams.

PLANNING

NON-FICTION WRITING PLAN

Decide on a topic and think about your target audience. The form of writing that you choose will be determined by the type of audience that you want to reach.

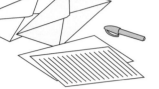

Think of an appropriate form: an article, essay, letter, etc.

Do the research: see experts who know the topic; go to libraries; use the Internet; look in encyclopedias; write to associated organisations.

Make notes on one side of pieces of paper and number the pages. Make a spidergram if you prefer. Instructions on how to produce a spidergram and an example are on pages 58–59.

Brainstorm

Look over your notes and plan your piece of writing on a single sheet. Number your points. Again this could be organised as a brainstorm.

Remember to write your title when you write or type your first draft. If you hand-write your work, leave every second line blank for proof-reading and alterations; it is easier to check your work that way. Always proof-read your work for spelling, punctuation and expression. Read the relevant pages in this book for advice.

Produce your best draft and remember to proof-read your work again for the errors that you are likely to make.

QUICK TEST

1. Identify a form of writing suitable for persuasive writing.

2. What does 'discursive' mean?

3. What is it that you are doing when you look over your work again?

4. How many drafts should you make of your work?

5. Identify three places where you could find information for your chosen topic.

Examiner's Top Tip
Always produce at least two drafts of your work. Your second draft should be your best one.

5. Libraries, encyclopedias, the Internet, knowledgeable people, associated organisations
4. At least two
3. Proof-reading
2. Rambling or digressive – passing from one subject to another
1. Leaflet or an article on an issue

HOW TO WRITE ESSAYS

Tips on how to get top marks when writing essays

1 PLANNING

- Examine <u>key</u> <u>words</u> and <u>phrases</u> in the question to help you focus on your answer.
- Read through your notes and any <u>important</u> <u>passages</u> in your text <u>for</u> <u>evidence</u>.
- <u>Brainstorm</u> an essay plan with your essay question in the middle of a blank piece of paper.
- <u>Aim</u> <u>for</u> <u>three</u> <u>or</u> <u>four</u> <u>main</u> <u>arguments</u> and group your points around them. Remember to include page numbers for any <u>quotations</u> used because you will need <u>evidence</u> <u>from</u> <u>your</u> <u>text(s)</u> to prove your <u>arguments</u>.

2 WRITING AN INTRODUCTION

Model introductions
Sometimes it is hard to start essays. A good way to begin is to answer the question briefly in your opening paragraph. Look at your notes and spidergrams to help you.

Example – An essay question for *Educating Rita*
Re-read the early and last scenes of *Educating Rita*. Explain what Rita gains and loses in her determination to become educated.

Educating Rita by Willy Russell tells the story of Rita White, a 26-year-old hairdresser, who is trying to 'find herself'. Rita's 'gains' can be summed up as follows:

The best place for your paragraph on historical context is shortly after your introduction; however it can come anywhere in the essay. This paragraph should be introduced like this:
'Rita is representative of many women in Britain in the late 1970s and 1980s who wanted to live fuller lives. They wanted the greater independence and real choices that could only be achieved through getting an education. However, Rita's experiences show that there were a number of obstacles that women had to face...'

3 THE MAIN BODY OF YOUR ESSAY

☆ Work through <u>each</u> <u>main</u> <u>argument</u> from your introduction as <u>fully</u> as you can.

☆ Once you think that you have proved an argument sufficiently, move on to your next argument. Do <u>not</u> hammer away at the same point for too long.

☆ Remember that your technique must be: <u>point</u>, <u>evidence</u> <u>and</u> <u>comment</u>.

☆ Use a wide range of <u>connective</u> <u>words</u> to link your points and arguments together. (See the spread on connective words on pages 20–21.) These words will join up your points and arguments and link your essay together; the skilful use of <u>connectives</u> can help the <u>fluency</u> <u>of</u> <u>arguments</u> in essays and make them easier to read.

Examiner's Top Tip
Get an idea of what good essays look like. Ask your teacher for good examples of work by former pupils.

4 CONCLUSION

Your essay needs to embody a sense of <u>finality</u>. This should be reflected in the tone of your conclusion.

Conclude by <u>summing</u> <u>up</u> your <u>arguments</u> and <u>findings</u>.

It may be that you have found an alternative way of understanding the question.

Maybe you will have discovered something that needs more <u>research</u>.

It is important to explain what you <u>learned</u> from writing your essay. Give <u>your</u> <u>views</u> on the <u>text(s)</u> that you are writing about.

Examiner's Top Tip
When you begin your essay do not put things off. We often find reasons not to write by doing almost anything else. Get started and fill up those blank pages! You can always correct and improve your work later on.

QUICK TEST

1. What should you focus on in essay questions?

2. What does 'text' mean?

3. What does a text's 'historical context' mean?

4. How many main arguments should you aim for?

5. Where do you give your personal opinion in an essay?

1. Understanding the whole question and paying attention to key words and phrases   2. Any book, play or poem in any genre   3. The period in which the text was written and what was going on at the time   4. Three or four   5. At the end and nowhere else

THE MEDIA

NEAB sets a coursework assignment on the media. All the exam boards include questions on a published form of the media in the final exams.

TERMS TO WORK INTO YOUR WRITING ON NEWSPAPERS

Earn higher grades by including these terms in your comments.

- **Break**: when the story emerges. Sometimes this is called 'breaking news'.
- **Byline**: gives the name of the journalist who wrote the piece.
- **Caption**: words which explain pictures or artwork.
- **Column**: a vertical article that appears on a page. This can be known as a 'leg'.
- **Copy**: written material submitted for publishing to the editor.
- **Diary column**: either a gossip column or a day-to-day personal column.
- **Down-page**: a name given to a story which appears in the bottom half of a newspaper page.
- **Editorial**: this can be all non-advertising copy. It can also be a column in which the newspaper expresses its opinion on a topic.
- **Exclusive**: a story carried by only one newspaper.
- **Eye-witness reporting**: where the reporter has been at an event.
- **Feature**: a distinct news story. This will give more background information from a wider range of resources than an eyewitness report. The journalist's opinion will be more apparent too.
- **Filler**: a short story of one or two paragraphs, used to fill space when a long story runs short.
- **Hard news**: news which looks at 'who', 'what', 'where', 'when' and 'why'. It is based on factual details with only a little description, journalistic comment or analysis.
- **Human-interest story**: this concentrates on tragedy, success, failure, or someone's emotional or sexual history.
- **In-depth reporting**: covers issues in some detail.
- **Lead**: the main story on the page. If this appears on the front page it is sometimes known as a 'splash'.
- **Punch-line**: the main point of a story.
- **Running story**: a story carried over several editions or days.
- **Soft news**: a light news story that is more colourful, witty and carries more commentary than hard news.
- **Tots**: is short for 'Triumph Over Tragedy Story'. These are popular as human-interest stories.

Examiner's Top Tip
Find out what the word 'text' means and use the term in your writing.

LAYOUT AND PRESENTATION

Below are some useful definitions.
- Artwork: all illustrations, such as cartoons, charts or maps.
- Banner: a front-page headline which spans the top of the page.
- Breaker: any device that breaks up text on a page, such as a cross-head or panel.
- Broadsheet: a larger newspaper often referred to as a 'quality' paper, such as *The Guardian* and *The Times,* aimed at an educated audience.
- Centre-spread: copy (written material) and pictures running over the middle pages of a newspaper.
- Classified ads: small adverts classified according to subject area and without illustrations.
- Colour: for sections of the paper printed on coloured paper such as finance. This can also be used to highlight the views of a journalist or simply descriptions or impressions.
- Crop: to cut a picture down.
- Cross-head: a small heading, normally of one or two words within a text that is often in a larger size of type.
- Display ads: large adverts often with illustrations; they can appear on the editorial pages.
- Layout: the design and look of the page.
- Masthead: the newspaper's title at the top of the front page.
- Mug shot: a photo just showing a person's face and sometimes their shoulders.
- Tabloid newspapers: refers to the smaller size of papers like *The Mirror, The Sun* or *The Express*.

HOW YOU WILL BE GRADED

You will be assessed on your ability to read and understand texts (including advertisements, articles, scripts for film, television and radio and any printed material published by the media) <u>as well as write about them</u>. You should aim to:

- express your <u>ideas</u>, <u>opinions</u> and <u>attitudes</u> as <u>impersonally</u> as you can. For example, use 'It seems', or 'the character appears' . . .rather than 'I think', etc. Remember to use the personal pronoun 'I' for what you think only at the end of essays
- give <u>detailed</u> ideas and points of view
- show that you can make <u>fine distinctions</u> between points of view
- <u>analyse</u> (unravel) points in texts as you discuss them
- show how <u>language</u> is used in media texts
- make <u>sustained</u> and <u>detailed</u> points on the effectiveness of layout in texts
- apply <u>appropriate</u> media terms effectively for your chosen text
- <u>compare</u> media texts.

WHAT YOU WILL BE EXPECTED TO DO

For your coursework assignment you will be expected to **analyse**, **review** and **comment** on features of a media text from such as magazines, radio, television programmes and films. Suitable tasks could include:

- an **examination of a news event** and an analysis of attitudes and bias in the way the news event is reported in different sections of the media such as television, radio and newspapers
- a **written account of a practical activity** in which you explain how you made a film, radio interview/show, or produced the front page for a newspaper
- comparing and contrasting **two soap operas from different countries**
- analysing a **full-page glossy advertisement from a magazine or newspaper**
- planning and producing **a television advert for a product such as a children's toy.**

A FRAMEWORK FOR LOOKING AT TEXTS

To make your analysis, ask the following questions:

Who <u>speaks</u> <u>this</u> <u>text</u>?
- Who is the 'I' or 'we' in the text?

Who <u>is</u> <u>the</u> <u>intended</u> <u>audience</u>?
- Who is expected to hear or read the text?

What <u>kind</u> <u>of</u> <u>text</u> <u>is</u> <u>it</u>?
- Does the text have a recognis-able form, such as an article or a leaflet?

What <u>does</u> <u>the</u> <u>text</u> <u>want</u>?
- <u>What</u> <u>are</u> <u>the</u> <u>writer's</u> <u>intentions</u>?
Are the purposes openly stated? What is the expected response?

What <u>does</u> <u>the</u> <u>text</u> <u>mean</u> <u>to</u> <u>me</u>?
- <u>What</u> <u>are</u> <u>my</u> <u>motives</u> for reading it?
How have I understood the text?

Do <u>I</u> <u>share</u> <u>its</u> <u>values</u>?
- What has it made me think about?

Examiner's Top Tip
When you study a media text remember that you are being assessed on your reading as well as your writing skills.

QUICK TEST

1. What is a centre-spread in a newspaper?

2. What is 'hard news'?

3. What is a 'running story'?

4. Who might be the audience for a broadsheet?

5. What is a tabloid?

6. What are the classifieds?

6. Small adverts that are classified according to subject area
5. A smaller-format newspaper like *The Sun*
4. An educated audience
3. A story that runs for days in several editions
2. Factual news, with little description, comment or analysis
1. Copy: written material and pictures running over the middle pages of a newspaper

HOW TO ANALYSE, REVIEW AND COMMENT ON A MEDIA TEXT (EN2/3)

Examiner's Top Tip
Always consider the purpose and target audience of a text before deciding on how its message is driven home.

- Only the best writers of English are hired to write the persuasive letters and information leaflets that pop through your letterbox. What follows are some of the clever ways they persuade or inform us.
- Use junk mail or an information leaflet from your doctor's waiting room or the public library and assess how something is explained or how you are persuaded to part with your money. Find examples of how advertisers try and inform or persuade you in media texts and write about them in a logical way. Try to say something about language first and then layout.

USE OF LANGUAGE TO PERSUADE OR INFORM

- Alliteration and exaggeration are often found in adverts and newspaper headlines. Writers use this to make something sound really enticing or awful. For example, 'Best-Ever Sale Starts Saturday'.

- Boxes are another helpful way of making information accessible.

- Bullet points do the same job: they also give the impression of being evidence; bullet points can also make complex information easy to understand.

- Emotive language is language which tries to get the reader to feel a particular emotion. Comparisons in writing that involve imagery can be surprisingly persuasive. 'For Lydia, life began on the scrap heap . . .' Look out for similes and the metaphor in the example.

- Informal language is made up of casual or shortened words which help create a chatty, friendly tone: 'info', 'sorted', 'nifty', 'piccies', 'mate' etc. This can also include local dialect: 'Watcha mate!'; 'ow's it goin'?'

- Interviews or personal accounts. The personal angle often helps us understand issues in ways that a general account will not. Newspapers and charities know that they can touch and persuade us with personal accounts of an experience: 'Jill lived in a cardboard box for two years.' This is because these organisations know that most people can empathise with the suffering of a single person or a family far better than with that of many thousands of people. News organisations and charities know that we are far more capable of understanding the particular rather than the abstract. Quotations also come into this category when given as evidence.

- Lists of facts also help us to understand the issues. They help support the pleader's case.

- Personal testimony from the famous or experts helps sell products. If David Ginola recommends you use Head and Shoulders, why shouldn't you?

- Questions are used to make you think; sometimes they are rhetorical questions to which no direct answer is expected: 'Now how could you object to that?'

- Repetition is the repeated words or phrases which emphasise a message. 'Fact: there are x number of homeless. Fact: 50 per cent are under the age of x.'

- Slogans can be titles to articles. They are usually catchy and memorable. They can play on well-known catch phrases. For example, 'A dog is for life', 'Cruelty to Children Must Stop!' and 'It's good to talk'.

- The use of the friendly second person such as 'You' or 'Dear Friend' and 'Dear Homeowner'. Look out for a signature at the end of any letters; this is meant as a personal touch and is sometimes in a different colour for extra effect.

PRESENTATION – LAYOUT TO PERSUADE OR INFORM

- **CAPITAL LETTERS CAN BE USED TO HIGHLIGHT IMPORTANT POINTS.**

- <u>Graphs</u> <u>and</u> <u>diagrams</u> make difficult information easy to grasp, especially comparisons, and they also break up forbidding blocks of writing.

- <u>Headings</u> are always important and are often well thought out; watch out for <u>alliteration</u> <u>or</u> <u>similes</u> <u>and</u> <u>metaphors</u> used to drive home points or messages. Here are a few <u>headlines</u> that should never have made it past their editors.

CAUSE OF AIDS FOUND – SCIENTISTS

THUGS EAT AND ROB PROPRIETOR!

Crack found in Australia

- **<u>Fonts</u>** <u>and</u> <u>colours</u> are always carefully chosen. Think about what is implied by the <u>fonts</u> and <u>colours</u> in <u>adverts</u> and <u>logos</u>. Look carefully at packaging, such as a cornflakes packet, and try to detect any subtle messages meant to reinforce public perceptions of the product.

- ***Italics*** *usually identify and emphasise crucial pieces of information.*

- **<u>Logos</u>** **<u>are</u>** **<u>symbols</u>** which represent and identify a company or charity. They can evoke strong messages or ideas and are usually very well thought out.

S

- <u>Maps</u> are useful for finding venues such as tourist attractions.

- <u>Catchy</u> <u>paragraph</u> <u>headings</u> summarise important information immediately in case you do not read the entire piece. They can also persuade you to read on.

- <u>Pictures</u> <u>and</u> <u>images</u> bring texts to life. A well-chosen picture of a child or an animal can tug at your heartstrings and <u>persuade</u> you to give money. Pictures also help break up blocks of writing and invite the reader to linger and find meaning.

- <u>Captions</u> help us understand pictures and interpret the images in the way the advertiser wants us to.

- <u>The</u> <u>use</u> <u>of</u> <u>colour</u> <u>in</u> <u>pictures</u> <u>and</u> <u>text</u> can reinforce messages and feelings about what you are reading. **Black** is the colour for death and seriousness, **white** is the colour for purity. **Red** is a warm, passionate colour as well as the colour for danger. **Blue** is a cold colour and it evokes the sea or freshness. Look again at your packets of washing powder and at the packaging of grocery items that you may never have consciously thought about before. There is usually a reason for the colours and fonts used on each of them.

- <u>Underlining is another way of emphasising a point and influencing the reader.</u>

QUICK TEST

1. What is the purpose of an advert from a charity?

a) to entertain b) inform/persuade c) evaluate?

2. How do writers create an informal tone?

3. What is emotive language?

4. What is the 'second person' in texts?

5. Why do writers from the media use graphs and diagrams?

6. What is the descriptive comment under a picture called?

Examiner's Top Tip
The skills that you learn regarding persuasive language and layout in the media will help you in your final exams on non-fiction texts. Remember to revise this section again during your final revision.

1. To inform/persuade
2. They use abbreviated and informal language or dialect
3. Language meant to evoke feelings in readers, probably using metaphors and similes
4. 'You', 'Dear Friend' etc.
5. To break down information to make it easier to understand
6. A caption

HOW TO BEGIN YOUR ESSAY

CHOOSE YOUR ADVERT

- <u>Choose</u> <u>an</u> <u>interesting</u>, <u>colourful</u>, <u>full-page</u> <u>advert</u> <u>from</u> <u>a</u> <u>magazine</u> and work out how the advertisers persuade their target audience to buy their product. How do they get their message across and how successful are they in doing so?
- Tick the points that apply to your chosen advert and work through the points as fully as you can.

YOUR ESSAY TITLE

The following information should be included in the title of your media essay:
- the name of the product
- the name of the advertiser or maker of the product
- the name and date of the magazine or newspaper where you found the advert.

A typical essay title could be worded as follows:

An analysis of a magazine advert for a Vaio laptop by Sony. The product was advertised in *The Observer Life Magazine* on 25 February 2001.

INTRODUCTION

Explain briefly what you are going to write about:
- the main subject(s) of the advert; that is the product and any models associated with it
- the advertisement's layout; that is, the overall appearance of the advert on the page
- the persuasive techniques used in the advert
- the intended target audience of the advert.

Examiner's Top Tip
Use standard English in formal essays. Avoid dialect unless it is called for.

WHO IS THE TARGET AUDIENCE FOR THE ADVERT?

- **Who is the advert aimed at? Give their age, sex, class, lifestyle, etc. The target audience will have a major influence on how the advert is set out and promoted.**

DESCRIBE THE MAIN SUBJECTS OF THE ADVERT

- *Examine the <u>status</u> and <u>appearance</u> of the product and the models that are associated with it.*

- *<u>Give</u> <u>details</u> about the main model's age, clothing, style, hair, etc. Examine the body language of the models (their facial expressions, eye contact, activity, pose, etc.).*

- *<u>What</u> <u>is</u> <u>the</u> <u>photographic</u> <u>coding</u> <u>of</u> <u>the</u> <u>advert</u>? (This refers to its framing, focus, angle, shading, effects and lighting.) Most adverts are <u>back-lit</u>; but other important strong lights include <u>key</u> and <u>filler</u> <u>lights</u> which are positioned to the side of the camera. These lights are usually trained on the models or on the product to make them appear bright and to avoid shadows. Think about the effects that can occur when one or more of these lights are switched off from the front, rear or side. For example, a shaded part of the advert would give a mysterious tone or feel to the advert and this would be a deliberate effect. <u>Lighting</u> is often used to create <u>mood</u> and <u>atmosphere</u>.*

- *<u>Examine</u> <u>any</u> <u>objects</u> <u>in</u> <u>the</u> <u>advert</u> and look just as carefully at the <u>background</u>. What do you think is the <u>purpose</u> of any <u>objects</u> or <u>signs</u> which may be in the <u>background</u> of the advert? Companies spend a lot of money on these adverts. Nothing is there by chance!*

- *The <u>context</u> (where and when) of the advert. Where does the advert fit in with the magazine in which it appears? What kind of story does it appear beside? Is there a link with an article? Does it allude to a topical event? Is the advert set in the present, future or past?*

DESCRIBE THE ADVERT'S LAYOUT

- Think about the use of <u>colour</u>. What do the colours used suggest? Has colour any <u>symbolic significance</u> in the advert?

- Comment on any other <u>graphic devices</u> that are present in your chosen advertisement. Suggest why they are there.

- How is <u>space</u> used within the advert? Does the model or product fill all the available space? Why or why not? What might be suggested by <u>empty spaces</u>?

- What is the <u>typography</u> of the advert? That is, the use of <u>type size, type style, fonts</u>, etc.

A MEDIA ESSAY TO ANALYSE AN ADVERT (EN2/3)

This will show you how to analyse an advert from a magazine. It could also help you catch up with your course-work or improve on an earlier media assignment.

ASSESS YOUR ADVERT'S PERSUASIVE TECHNIQUES

- its <u>genre</u> and <u>conventions</u>. In other words, what types of people are shown and <u>how are they presented</u>? Is the scene filled with secret agents, business people, pop stars, gamblers, etc. or does the advert try to recreate romantic or thrilling scenes, Victorian times, modern living or the future? <u>How is the chosen genre persuasive</u>?

- any <u>celebrities</u> or <u>personalities</u> used and what they are normally associated with. Does the advertised product feed off <u>any associations</u> with these celebrities?

- any <u>hard information</u>: facts, figures, etc.

- promises of <u>pleasure</u>. What good things could result from buying the product?

Write about any of the following that apply to your advert

- any <u>figures of speech</u>, including puns or double meanings, personification, alliteration, etc.

- any sense of <u>belonging</u>: are you expected to identify with any group, class, trend, etc.?

- <u>expert witnesses</u> or <u>personal testimony</u> and what is gained from their use

- <u>scientific jargon</u>: unusual words and terms that are meant to impress <u>an audience</u>

- any appeals to your <u>conscience</u>: emotional blackmail, lifestyle, commitments

- any <u>advantageous promises</u>: freebies, coupons, improved lifestyle, freedom, sexual attractiveness

- repetition with the <u>rule of three</u> to help emphasise points

Examiner's Top Tip
If you get stuck on any of the points for this essay just ask your teacher. That is what he or she is there for.

CONCLUSION

- Say whether you think your chosen advert is <u>successful</u> in its aims. If you think that it was, briefly sum up why. You could recycle the most interesting findings of your essay here.

- Explain what you have <u>learned</u> through writing this essay and <u>give your final views</u> on advertisers and the methods that they use through advertising agencies to persuade us to buy their products.

HOW TO WRITE ABOUT A TV ADVERT (EN2/3)

OTHER POINTS TO CONSIDER ON TV ADVERTS

Look back at the previous spread to see the methods which advertisers use to persuade us on paper. Which of these can be applied to TV adverts?

OTHER CAMERA SHOTS WHICH HELP TELL A STORY

- CUTS: changes of scenes from one setting to another.
- DISSOLVE: where one scene dissolves into another.
- WIPE: where one scene is wiped from the screen by another.
- MONTAGE, otherwise known as 'rapid editing': a number of camera shots that follow each other in quick succession to create an effect. This type of approach is usually used alongside a soundtrack. A good, recent example of this is the stunningly dramatic opening of *Romeo and Juliet* (1996) starring Leonardo Di Caprio and Clare Danes.
  If you find montage being used in your advert, the main question that you need to ask is Why? What is the purpose behind the effect?

MORE STORY-LINE FEATURES TO THINK ABOUT

- The use of narrative to entertain viewers. Is the advert a one-off or one of a series? Either way, what is the story line of the advert? How does it help sell the product?

- Stereotypes can be used as a means for quick understanding: working/careworn housewives, unattractive traffic wardens, etc. Given the time restrictions on an advert, such use of shorthand for instant understanding is inevitable. Do they help sell the product?

- The choice of setting: workplace, bar, home, market, imaginary, etc. Is the advert set in the present, future or past? Does the setting have any bearing on the persuasiveness of the advert?

- The use of a particular genre: spy, thriller, musical, adventure, romantic comedy, etc. Again, does this sell the product? What persuasive associations can you draw from the advertiser's chosen genre?

- What values seem to be within and outside the adverts? Is there anything in it that we are expected to agree with? Look out for values that suggest 'family life', 'law and order', 'making money', 'being an individual', 'freedom', etc.

- How music and sound are used to create mood and atmosphere. Is the music realistically part of the background, say coming from a jukebox (diagetic sound) or is it deliberately inserted into the advert (non-diagetic sound)? What is the effect of using each type of sound? How does the sound add to the persuasiveness of the advert?

- The use of voice-overs. Voices to endorse products can also help create a mood and atmosphere. The voices can suggest sexually charged women, reassuring males or convincing experts and may be provided by celebrities.

- The use of increased volume. It sometimes seems that the volume goes up on some commercial television channels the instant the adverts come on! Perhaps the advertiser want to ensure that you heard their message even if you have left the room. Advertisers seem to be using this technique more and more.

- Who the target audience could be. This will be determined by when the advert is shown and the programmes shown during commercial breaks and after the advert.

CHOOSE AN ADVERT THAT INTERESTS YOU AND RECORD IT

<u>Examine</u> <u>the</u> <u>methods</u> <u>through</u> <u>which</u> <u>the</u> <u>advertiser</u> <u>tries</u> <u>to</u> <u>persuade</u> <u>you</u> <u>to</u> <u>buy</u> <u>a</u> <u>product</u> <u>or</u> <u>use</u> <u>a</u> <u>service</u>. Look carefully at some television adverts and notice how the <u>shot-building</u> occurs. This, taken together with how camera shots are <u>framed</u>, is part of the '<u>grammar</u>' of the film. Much of what follows could be applied to any movie assignments that you have been set.

The usual rule for camera work in television is that there are <u>no</u> <u>more</u> <u>than</u> <u>two</u> <u>people</u> <u>in</u> <u>a</u> <u>room</u>. If there are more than two characters in a room then the camera tends to focus on only two of them.

Here are a number of <u>basic</u> <u>terms</u> to consider when you do your research.
Use them as you make points in your essays and show how they add
meaning to the <u>persuasiveness</u> of an advert.

SHOT-MAKING WITH A CAMERA

Camera shots help tell a story <u>visually</u> and they contribute towards <u>mood</u> <u>and</u> <u>atmosphere</u>. They often build up to <u>close-ups</u> and then back to <u>half</u> <u>shots</u> and <u>total</u> <u>shots</u> as scenes reach a level of <u>dramatic</u> <u>intensity</u> and then fall away. <u>You</u> <u>could</u> <u>have</u>, <u>say</u>, <u>an</u> <u>establishing</u> <u>shot</u>, <u>two</u> <u>total</u> <u>shots</u>, <u>four</u> <u>mid</u> <u>shots</u>, <u>six</u> <u>close-ups</u> <u>and</u> <u>then</u> <u>back</u> <u>to</u> <u>four</u> <u>mid</u> <u>shots</u> <u>followed</u> <u>by</u> <u>two</u> <u>total</u> <u>shots</u> etc. It is a bit like composing music.

- <u>Establishing</u> shot: this shot locates <u>time</u> <u>and</u> <u>place</u>. For example if the action switches to an airport, the camera shows us shots of planes landing to tell us that the scene is now at an airport.

- <u>Long</u> shot or <u>total</u> shot: this shows <u>the</u> <u>whole</u> <u>body</u> and lets you know who is important in the advert.

- <u>Mid</u> shot: this shows the chest and shoulders. It shows <u>who</u> <u>is</u> <u>talking</u> and who is <u>significant</u> in a scene.

- <u>Close-Up</u>: this is an expressive shot for the director. <u>It</u> <u>can</u> <u>show</u> <u>emotion</u> of all kinds. <u>Extreme</u> <u>close-ups</u> might show only a mouth, for example.

- <u>Pan</u> shot: the camera swivels from one thing to another.

- <u>Pull</u> <u>focus</u>: the depth of field or <u>background</u> changes from one character or part of a set to another.

- <u>Point</u> <u>of</u> <u>view</u>: a camera shot from the point of view of a character. This camera shows what a character would see. In other words, the camera substitutes for the character.

- <u>High-angle</u> <u>shots</u>: these shots tend to look down on someone or a <u>scene</u>. They show power for the viewer and vulnerability for the person looked upon. They can be related to the <u>point</u> <u>of</u> <u>view</u> – and thus power – of another <u>character</u>. The effect is similar with a <u>low-angle</u> <u>shot</u> in which a character seems powerless, having to look up at someone above them.

Examiner's Top Tip
Use as many technical terms as you can in your essays. Remember to use them effectively with evidence and not just because you have heard them.

QUICK TEST

1. What is a point-of-view shot?

2. What is an establishing shot?

3. Where would you expect to see an establishing shot in a programme?

4. What emotions can a high-angle shot bring out?

5. What is the ideal number of characters in a scene for television?

6. What is meant by a 'stereotype'?

7. What is the significance of a long shot?

7. It introduces the significant characters in a scene.
6. When we see people as types and not as individuals
5. Two (it is an unwritten rule in television)
4. A sense of power for the one looking down, vulnerability for anyone looking up
3. At the beginning of a programme and every time a major change of scene happens
2. The shot sets the scene and lets the audience know where the action is taking place.
1. The camera shows what a particular character can see.

EXAM QUESTIONS - Use the questions to test your progress. Check your answers on page 94.

Original Writing

1. Will you be assessed on writing or reading?

....

2. What is the word length that you should be aiming at?

....

3. What does 'narrative' mean?

....

4. What does 'genre' mean?

....

5. Similes are comparisons. How do they differ from metaphors?

....

6. What does 'hook' mean in terms of stories?

....

7. What is meant by 'setting'?

....

8. Give two examples of what you could write about as an assignment.

....

9. What does 'original writing' mean?

....

10. What are the main styles of narration?

....

11. If a narrator is outside the story, what is he or she?

....

12. What does 'plot' mean?

....

13. Give a method by which you can plan your story.

....

14. Explain what is meant by 'control' in writing.

....

15. If writing is linear what is it?

....

Personal Writing: Non-fiction

16. What does non-fiction mean?

....

17. Give two examples of what you could write about.

....

18. If your task is 'discursive', how is it written?

....

19. Give three sources where you could find information on a topic.

....

20. Will an imaginative story be suitable for a non-fiction assignment?

....

21. What does 'target audience' mean?

....

22. Identify three forms that you could use for persuasive writing.

....

23. What is meant by the term 'text'?

....

24. Name a text that 'informs' or 'advises'.
....

25. Is biography a form of non-fiction?
....

26. If you are asked to 'compare' and 'contrast' what are you expected to do?
....

27. What is meant by the 'historical context' of a text?
....

28. Briefly explain what you need to do to write an essay.
....

29. Where do you put your personal views in an essay?
....

30. Explain what 'Point—Evidence—Comment' means.
....

The Media

31. What does the term 'media' include?
....

32. Identify a task that you could do as a media assignment.
....

33. Explain these terms from 'Layout and Presentation':
a) artwork..
b) broadsheet..
c) layout..
d) mug-shot..
e) display ads..

34. Explain these terms from 'Your Writing on Newspapers':
a) byline..
b) exclusive..
c) human-interest story..
d) punch-line..
e) lead story..

35. Give three of five questions that you should ask of any non-fiction text.
....

36. Find and give an example of emotive language from a leaflet or advert promoted by a charity.
....

37. What is a slogan? Write down two examples.
....

38. Why do companies create logos?
....

39. Give two examples of how writers use presentation and layout to emphasise their points.
....

40. Give an example of the 'second person'.
....

How did you do?

1–10	correct	.....................start again
11–20	correct	..................getting there
21–30	correct	.................good work
31–40	correct	................excellent

WHAT YOU MAY STUDY

This will be determined by what your English teachers have in their stock cupboard; you'll probably get to study what Year 9 have not been set for their SATs! If you are lucky there will be a recent film of the play that you can rent which will help your overall understanding of it.

As you read the play try to get the gist of what characters are saying before you read passages again for a more detailed understanding. Make use of any general notes in your books to guide your understanding as well.

The plays you are most likely to study are:

Antony and Cleopatra
Henry IV Part One or *Two*
Henry V
Julius Caesar
The Merchant of Venice
Romeo and Juliet

Macbeth
A Midsummer's Night's Dream
The Tempest
Twelfth Night
The Winter's Tale

Examiner's Top Tip
To understand Shakespeare aim to get a rough idea of what is going on. Once you have this you can then deepen your understanding by reading for more meaning in imagery and word choices. A good exercise to attune yourself to the language is to translate six-line passages into modern English.

THE SHAKESPEARE ASSIGNMENT

HOW YOU WILL BE GRADED

To achieve grades C to A* you will need to show that you are able to do some of the following.

1. You will show through your critical and personal response how meaning is made in the play.

2. You will be expected to support your points with textual evidence on the play's language, themes, characters or structure.

3. You should show that you understand the play and the implications from its themes and relevance for what people thought important in Shakespeare's day and in our time. Interpretations of texts can change over time as people read them in accordance with the values and ideas of their time.

4. In some of your comments you should show an awareness of Shakespeare's linguistic devices: his use of imagery through metaphors, similes, personification, alliteration, oxymorons, etc.

5. Try to say something about the play's philosophical context and how the play sits within its dramatic genre. The philosophical context means the values and ideas that were thought important when the play was written. An hour or two with an up-to-date history book of the time would help you find these things out.

6. You should give detailed and sustained analysis of Shakespeare's use of language for poetic, figurative, and dramatic effect and develop your points.

7. Try, if you can, to show an awareness of alternative interpretations in your writing.

WHAT YOU HAVE TO DO

You will need to show that you <u>understand</u> the play and can engage with it in an essay or a piece of writing.

If your essay or writing is going be used to count for your Literature GCSE you'll also need to show an awareness of <u>the background</u> to the play. That is, the <u>historical, cultural</u> and <u>literary traditions which shaped</u> Shakespeare's <u>play</u>. The best place to include such <u>background</u> is in the early part of your essay.

YOU COULD:

*   <u>write an essay on a character, themes</u> or <u>structure</u> of the play
*   <u>examine the dramatic qualities</u> of one or more scenes
*   <u>write a commentary</u> after hot-seating or role-playing a character from your play
*   <u>write a character study</u>
*   <u>analyse the dramatic effects</u> of <u>imagery</u> or other language features in the play
*   <u>write about a performance</u> of <u>the play</u> from the theatre, television or film.

Examiner's Top Tip
As with any writer, when you write essays on Shakespeare you should use the P.E.C. method:
*   make a point
*   give evidence for your point
*   comment on your evidence.

SHAKESPEARE'S CHOICE OF LANGUAGE

Shakespeare used <u>three styles of writing</u> in his plays. Here are a few examples from Twelfth Night*:*

1. <u>Poetic verse (Rhymed)</u> Often used to signal the end of scenes like a curtain call or for heightened dramatic effect. Take, for example, this rhyming couplet from Twelfth Night*:*

Duke Orsino: *Away before me to sweet beds of flowers:*
Love-thoughts lie rich when canopied with bowers.

2. <u>Blank verse (Unrhymed)</u> Verse which was intended to represent the rhythms of speech. It is usually used by noble characters who are given elevated speech to show their feelings and mood:

Duke Orsino: *If music be the food of love play on.*

Note how the speech is in <u>iambic pentameter</u>. That is, it has 10 syllables to the line in which five are <u>stressed</u>. The <u>rhythm pattern</u> is ti-tum, ti-tum, ti-tum, ti-tum, ti-tum. Sometimes you'll find more or fewer <u>stresses</u> to the lines yet the overall pattern will be even in the end.

3. <u>Prose</u> Ordinary language used by characters of all ranks. Uneducated characters tend to use it. It can also be used for comic exchanges between characters, for plot development and for speech which lacks dramatic intensity:

Viola as Cesario: *Save thee, friend, and thy music.*
Dost thou live by thy tabor?
Feste: *No, sir, I live by the church.*
Viola: *Art thou a churchman?*
Feste: *No such matter sir: I do live by the church;*
for I do live at my house, and my house
doth stand by the church.

Twelfth Night

QUICK TEST

1. Give an example of a Shakespeare assignment that you could do.
2. What is 'textual evidence'?
3. Why does Shakespeare use blank verse?
4. Why does Shakespeare use poetic verse?

4. For moments of high drama and intense feeling
3. It is elevated speech and it invests its speakers with dignity. Nobles, for example, often use it.
2. Brief quotations from the play that are used as evidence for points in essays
1. Write an essay; you could also, for example, write the stage directions of a director for a scene or two of a play.

THE STRUCTURE AND THEMES OF SHAKESPEARE'S PLAYS

This typical structure or plot of a Shakespeare play is oversimplified, but this basic framework should help you see how the play that you are studying is set out.

SOME RECURRING THEMES, IDEAS OR MESSAGES

CONFLICT
Macbeth, Julius Caesar, Romeo and Juliet, Antony and Cleopatra, The Merchant of Venice, Henry IV Parts I and II and Henry V.

VARIOUS FORMS OF LOVE AND LOYALTY
Twelfth Night, Romeo and Juliet, A Midsummer Night's Dream, The Merchant of Venice, Antony and Cleopatra and The Winter's Tale.

CHANGE
Characters in most plays. Some characters such as Malvolio (Twelfth Night) and Shylock (The Merchant of Venice), are punished because they cannot change.

FATE
Most plays; <u>also</u> <u>the</u> <u>role</u> <u>of</u> <u>the</u> <u>individual</u> <u>against</u> <u>society</u>.

FORTUNE
Every play. This is the notion of the Goddess of Fortune making and breaking us by giving or denying us luck.

ORDER, DISORDER AND STABILITY
Most plays. This is usually linked to <u>Nature</u>.

GOOD AND EVIL
Most plays.

APPEARANCE AND REALITY
Most comedies and some tragedies. The <u>themes</u> probably reflect the great changes in society during Shakespeare's time.

DISGUISE AND IDENTITY
Most comedies and some tragedies. The plays often depict the gap between what is said and how it is interpreted. Characters can deceitfully misuse words too.

SELF-KNOWLEDGE
This can be found in most comedies; however there is often one character, like Malvolio in Twelfth Night, who is incapable of accepting his faults and learning about himself.

KINGSHIP AND THE USE AND ABUSE OF POWER
Macbeth, Julius Caesar, Henry IV Parts I and II and Henry V.

JUSTICE
Several plays including The Merchant of Venice and Macbeth.

LOVE AND MARRIAGE
Several plays.

LIBRARIAN, MID-KENT COLLEGE OF HIGHER & FURTHER EDUCATION OAKWOOD PARK, TONBRIDGE ROAD MAIDSTONE, KENT ME16 8AQ

PLOT STRUCTURE

Shakespeare liked to stress the comedy or seriousness of many scenes within his plays by making <u>dramatic</u> <u>contrasts</u>. He did this by placing <u>a serious scene after a comic one</u> and vice versa.

- <u>Main characters are introduced to the audience</u>. Order reigns and the world and nature are in natural harmony.

- <u>Problems are revealed</u>. Things begin to go wrong. Confusions, murders, deceit, pranks and other complications begin.

- As events progress there is <u>chaos</u> and a <u>loss of order and harmony</u>. The natural world appears out of sorts.

- Things come to a head in the play's <u>climax</u>. ('Climax' comes from the Greek word for 'ladder'). If you are reading a <u>tragedy</u> then several more deaths occur now, including a main character like Macbeth. <u>The climax is the moment of the highest dramatic intensity</u> in the play, particularly for the main character.

- <u>Order</u> is <u>re-established</u> with the right people in control again. <u>Nature is again at one with the main characters</u>. Comedies usually end in several, usually three, marriages.

Examiner's Top Tip
Always be prepared to say what you think of the play that you studied. Your view is important and it should be expressed at the end of your essay.

QUICK TEST

1. What is a theme?
2. Where would you find the 'climax' of a play?
3. What does 'plot' mean?
4. What does 'context' mean?
5. Why would it be useful to see a performance of a Shakespeare play?

Examiner's Top Tip
Go to see a live performance of a play, if you can, because this will help your understanding of the play. Shakespeare intended his plays to be performed and not read when he wrote them.

5. It would help you understand the whole play and know how speeches could be interpreted. Shakespeare wanted his plays to be heard and seen, not just read.
4. The events and ideas around at the time when the text was written
3. The plan or outline of the play
2. Near the end
1. It is the play's main message or idea. There can be several themes in a play.

SHAKESPEARE'S IMAGERY

FIGURES OF SPEECH

Examiner's Top Tip
If the audience knows more about a development of the plot than the characters then this is known as dramatic irony.

Shakespeare uses <u>figures</u> <u>of</u> <u>speech</u> – that is, <u>imagery</u> or <u>word</u> <u>pictures</u> – to do the following:
- say more about points made in <u>dialogue</u> and <u>action</u>
- <u>reinforce</u> and <u>enhance</u> the <u>audience's</u> <u>ideas</u> of the <u>characters</u>
- <u>magnify</u> or <u>draw</u> <u>attention</u> to <u>themes/issues</u> in the text.

To do this he uses:

- <u>**similes**</u>: comparisons using '<u>as</u>' or '<u>like</u>': 'The moon is <u>like</u> a balloon.'

- <u>**personification**</u>: giving human feelings to animals or inanimate objects.

- <u>**metaphors**</u>: stronger comparisons saying something is something else: 'The moon is a balloon.'

- <u>**extended**</u> <u>**metaphors**</u>: a metaphor that is used extensively throughout a passage.

- <u>**oxymorons**</u>: these are <u>words</u> and <u>phrases</u> that you would not expect to see yoked together to cause an effect. As soon as Juliet hears that Tybalt, her cousin, has been killed by Romeo, her grief and outrage is tempered by her disbelief that Romeo could carry out such a deed:

'Fiend angelical, dove-feathered raven, wolvish-ravening lamb, ... A damned saint, an honourable villain!'
– *Romeo and Juliet*, Act 3, Scene 2, lines 75–79

- **motifs**: <u>characters</u>, <u>themes</u> or <u>images</u> which <u>recur</u> throughout a text. For example, <u>disguise</u> is a running idea in *Twelfth Night*. In *Macbeth* there are several <u>motifs</u>. One is '<u>fair</u> <u>and</u> <u>foul</u>' and another is <u>sleep</u>. To the Weird Sisters, who characterise evil, what is ugly is beautiful, and what is beautiful is ugly: 'Fair is foul and foul is fair.' Macbeth and Lady Macbeth reign in restless ecstasy after murdering King Duncan. Macbeth soon says to illustrate the sleep <u>motif</u>:

'Me thought I heard a voice cry, "Sleep no more!"
Macbeth does murder sleep — the innocent sleep,
Sleep that knits up the ravelled sleave of care,
The death of each day's life, sore labour's bath,
Balm of hurt minds, great nature's second course
Chief nourisher in life's feast.'
– *Macbeth*, Act 2, Scene 2, 34–39

Examiner's Top Tip
Keep quotations relevant and brief. Aim to use single words and phrases or no more than a sentence or so to prove your points. Remember to comment on the quotations that you use: your style should be P.E.C. (point – evidence – comment).

AN EXTENDED EXAMPLE OF SHAKESPEARE'S USE OF IMAGERY

In the following speech from *King Lear*, Kent is enquiring of a Gentleman whether Cordelia, the daughter of King Lear, has been upset by a letter describing her father's condition.

Kent	O, then it mov'd her?
Gentleman	Not to a rage. Patience and sorrow strove
	Who should express her goodliest. You have seen
	Sunshine and rain at once: her smiles and tears
	Were like a better way. Those happy smilets
	That play'd on her ripe lip seem'd not to know
	What guests were in her eyes, which parted thence
	As pearls from diamonds dropp'd. In brief,
	Sorrow would be a rarity most belov'd,
	If all could so become it.

King Lear, Act 4, Scene 3

The gentleman attempts to describe Cordelia's conflicting emotions in a number of ways. First he uses <u>personification</u> to make the struggle in her mind between patience and sorrow seem more vivid. He then moves on to <u>metaphors</u> of 'sunshine' and 'rain' to express these emotions. In order to give an impression of the strength of her emotions, he again uses personification to characterise the smilets (small smiles) that 'played' on her lips, and the tears that were 'guests' in her eyes. Finally, he uses a simile to describe the richness and beauty of Cordelia's tears, which part from her eyes as 'pearls from diamonds dropp'd'.

This moment is very moving. It is an example of Shakespeare's dramatic technique that he has Cordelia's reaction described rather than calling upon an actor to play it.

QUICK TEST

Examiner's Top Tip
Get a recording of a play from your local library and listen to parts of the play as it is read. It will help your understanding of the play.

Circle the correct answer:

1. A theme is:

    a) a song b) an idea/issue or message c) personification d) a character.

2. Shakespeare uses imagery to:

    a) make his writing pretty b) because he is vain c) fill up space d) enhance our understanding of a character, theme or a point.

3. A simile is a figure of speech which:

    a) draws a comparison using 'as' or 'like' b) allows characters to smile c) has to do with singularity d) makes a comparison using 'is' or 'are'?

4. The term 'imagery' means:

    a) looking in mirrors b) word pictures c) writing prose d) knitting.

5. The climax of a play is:

    a) its ending b) its beginning c) when the action comes to a head d) in the middle.

5. c
4. b
3. a
2. d
1. b

CALIBAN IN *THE TEMPEST*

Caliban is the son of the witch Sycorax and the original inhabitant of the island on which the play is set. As such, he represents some aspects of Elizabethan ideas of the noble savage.

When he arrived at the island, Prospero released Ariel from his captivity and attempted to 'civilise' Caliban. Unfortunately, Caliban proved unteachable and attempted to rape Miranda – see Act 1 Scene 2. The more sinister side of Caliban's name is suggested by its similarity to 'cannibal'.

Following his fall from grace, Caliban works as a servant for Prospero but feels that the island has been stolen from him (Act 1 Scene 2).

Caliban is not without redeeming features. He is sensitive to the natural world of the island and entranced by the noises and music he hears (Act 3 Scene 2).

On meeting Stephano and Trinculo, Caliban learns the joys of drink. He sees them as gods come to save him from the slavery of Prospero. They plan to kill Prospero but a quarrel breaks out thanks to an invisible Ariel. Caliban's plot is reported to Prospero and comes to nothing.

Caliban's ugliness is constantly emphasised. Miranda calls him an 'abhorred slave' whilst Trinculo and Stephano refer to him as a 'moon-calf' and a 'monster'.

Although Caliban is punished for his plot against Prospero, he is eventually given back his island.

CALIBAN'S ROLE WITHIN THE PLAY

Although Caliban has some comic scenes with Trinculo and Stephano, his encounters with Prospero reveal a sense of failure and powerlessness on the part of the magician. His attempts to educate Caliban have been repaid only with curses.

As the original inhabitant of the island, Caliban represents all the native people encountered by Europeans in the Elizabethan era of exploration. Through Caliban, Shakespeare explores the idea of the noble savage and questions the assumptions often made about them.

The play also explores the debate between nature and nurture. Caliban is evil in a way, but he has had none of the advantages of a European education. Antonio, on the other hand, is a sophisticated courtier who has had all the benefits of education and upbringing. Antonio, it turns out, is as inclined to evil and plotting as Caliban. To Antonio the island is nothing but a barren desert but to Caliban it is a place of enchantment.

CALIBAN'S APPEARANCE

Miranda	Tis a villain, sir, I do not love to look upon. (1, ii, 312)
Prospero	A freckled whelp hag-born – not honoured with A human shape. (1, ii, 282)
Prospero	Thou poisonous slave, got by the devil himself Upon thy wicked dam. (1, ii, 321)
Trinculo	What have we here? A man or a fish? Dead or alive? A fish: he smells like a fish; a very ancient and fish like smell. A strange fish! Legg'd like a man! And his fins like arms! (2, ii, 25)
Stephano	Have we devils here? Do you put tricks upon's with savages and men of Inde, ha? This is some monster of the isle... Where the devil did he learn our language?... An abominable monster! (2, ii, 58)

CALIBAN ON:

PROSPERO

I must obey: his Art is of such pow'r
It would control my dam's god, Setebos,
And make a vassal of him. (I, 2)

All the infections that the sun sucks up
From bogs, fens, flats, on Prosper fall, and make him
By inch-meal a disease! His spirits hear me...
For every trifle they are set upon me;
Sometimes like apes, that mow and chatter at me,
And after bite me; then like hedgehogs, which
Lie tumbling in my barefoot way, and mount
Their pricks at my footfall; sometime am I
All wound with adders, who with cloven tongues
Do hiss me into madness (II, 2)

MIRANDA

You taught me language, and my profit on't
Is, I know how to curse. The red plague rid you
    For learning me your language! (I, 2)

And that most deeply to consider is
The beauty of his daughter; he himself
Calls her a nonpareil. I never saw a woman
But only Sycorax my dam and she;
But she as far surpasseth Sycorax
As great'st does least. (III, 2)

TRINCULO

That's a brave god, and bears celestial liquor. I will
kneel to him. I do adore thee. I'll show thee every
fertile inch of the island; and I will kiss thy foot. I
prithee, be my god. (III, 2)

'Ban, 'Ban, Ca-Caliban
Has a new master, get a new man! (III, 2)

THE ISLAND

Be not afeard. The isle is full of noises,

Sounds, and sweet airs, that give delight, and hurt not.
Sometimes a thousand twangling instruments
Will hum about mine ears; and sometimes voices,
That, if I then had wak'd after long sleep,
Will make me sleep again; and then, in dreaming,
The clouds methought would open and show riches
Ready to drop upon me, that, when I wak'd,
I cried to dream again. (III, 2)

This island's mine, by Sycorax my mother,
Which thou tak'st from me. When thou came'st first,
Thou strok'st me, and made much of me; wouldst give me
Water with berries in't; and teach me how
To name the bigger light, and how the less,
That burn by day and night: and then I lov'd thee,
And show'd thee all the qualities of the isle,
The fresh springs, brine-pits, barren place and fertile:
Curs'd be I that did so! (I, 2)

ESSAY NOTES FOR CALIBAN'S ROLE AND FUNCTION IN *THE TEMPEST*

QUICK TEST

1. What are the main ways in which you can find out about a character?
2. Name the three main types of Shakespeare plays.
3. Why does Shakespeare have important characters speak soliloquies?

1. From what they say, what they do and from what others say about them you can discover more from any imagery associated with them.
3. Shakespeare mainly wrote history, tragedy and comedy plays.
4. Dramatists wrote soliloquies for important characters to help audiences understand the thoughts, feelings and motives of these characters.

Title: How does Shakespeare present Caliban in *The Tempest*? Is he a noble savage or just a savage?

The three steps in planning this essay are:
- **Read the question carefully and identify the key words**
- **Review the notes on the previous page**
- **Decide which material is relevant and how you are going to structure them.**

You can then plan your essay along the following lines.

Examiner's Top Tip
In order to get a high mark, you will need to include some comments on the cultural and historical context of the play that you have been asked to study.

Introduction – response to question and issues involved

Section 1
Arguments in favour of the idea that Caliban is just a savage
- Poor response to education.
- Attempt to rape Miranda.
- Hatred and fear of Prospero.
- Response to alcohol.
- Attitude to Trinculo – treats him as god.
- Attempt to overthrow Prospero.

Section 2
Arguments in favour of noble savage idea
- He is the original inhabitant of the island dispossessed by Prospero.
- His sensitivity to the island.
- 'Isle is full of noises' speech – sensitive nature.
- Self awareness shown when cursing Miranda for teaching him to speak.
- Compare his behaviour with Trinculo, Stephano and Antonio.

Section 3
Significance of Caliban's ugliness
- Surface only? Prejudice?
- Compare Antonio's rich clothes hiding deeper sin.

Section 4
Shakespeare's presentation – how the audience's sympathies are manipulated
- Introduced as servant.
- History explained in Act 1 Scene 2 – early innocent response turns sour.
- Sympathy for him because he is ruled by fear?
- Meeting with Trinculo and Stephano – comedy. Do we lose or gain sympathy when he chooses Trinculo as his new master?
- His innocence/ignorance – only seen two women. Compare Miranda's 'O brave new world'.
- Punishment by Ariel – is this excessive?
- Plot revealed – was he ever really a danger?

Shakespeare's language and theatrical techniques
- Caliban's curses – close analysis.
- More poetic speeches – close analysis.
- Costume issues. Compare Ariel.

Conclusion
- No easy answer – Caliban both noble and savage.
- Why you think Shakespeare doesn't make simple choice.
- Personal opinion.

Once you have planned your essay, you need to go back to the text to find suitable quotations and references. Sticky notes inserted in the book are a good idea at this stage.

Examiner's Top Tip
Proof-read your essay for punctuation, capital letters and clarity of expression. Remember to check the relevance of your points and arguments. Ask yourself, 'Have I answered the question?'

REFINING YOUR ARGUMENT

The introduction

Your <u>opening</u> <u>paragraph</u> should address the key points of the question. The most important word is '<u>present</u>' as it asks you not just to discuss whether or not Caliban is a savage but to talk about <u>how Shakespeare introduces and manipulates these ideas</u>. At this point, you can also explain how noble savages would have been interesting to an Elizabethan audience living in an age of exploration.

The body of the essay

This should be well <u>supported</u> <u>by</u> <u>quotations</u> and close references. You should <u>avoid retelling the story</u> of the play. Make sure that you comment on each part of the story in terms of its <u>effect on audience sympathy</u> in section 4.

Conclusion

You do not need to restate the whole argument but you should think in terms of what you have learned from writing the essay. You might like to consider:

- the balance between 'noble' and 'savage'
- why Shakespeare made a minor character like Caliban so bad and so good.

SUGGESTED ESSAY PLAN FOR SHAKESPEARE'S *THE TEMPEST*

For improved expression in your arguments look at the linking words and phrases section on pages 20–21 to help you signpost your argument. Try to link your ideas together and make connections between your points wherever you can.

INTERNET

Web sites for help with Shakespeare plays
Mr. William Shakespeare and the Internet:
http://shakespeare.palomar.edu/
Another good one with some study guides is
Absolute Shakespeare:
http://absoluteshakespeare.com/index.htm

HOW TO PRODUCE SPIDERGRAMS FOR ESSAYS

RE-READ YOUR TEXT

Whether you are reading a play, novel or short story, **you must** re-read your text **for a deeper understanding of your** essay question or task. **Many teachers concentrate on scenes from plays and chapters from novels for written assignments.** In plays **they expect pupils to focus on** dramatic technique. **For example, you may be asked to** show how dramatic tension is created in a particular scene. In novels **you might be expected to show how a** theme, character, imagery or mood, **has been represented. One of the best ways of making notes for your essay is to produce a** memorable spidergram. **Study your essay question or task and** try to build up relevant comments by looking carefully at key words and phrases in your question.

WHEN TO USE A SPIDERGRAM

If your essay title asks you to write about a character, theme or any aspect of a text that you are studying, you could do a spidergram like the one on the opposite page. Study your essay question and try to build up relevant comments by looking carefully at key words and phrases in your question. Check your ideas again by rereading key parts of the text.

Examiner's Top Tip
The habit of producing spidergrams or brainstorms that focus on three or four main points will help you plan your answers when you take the final exams.

STUDY THE CHARACTERS

You can learn about characters by examining:
- *what they say*
- *what they do*
- *what other characters say about them*
- *stage directions*
- *how they develop (that is, do they change or do they remain the same? If so, why?)*

BUILD YOUR SPIDERGRAM AS YOU READ

Go through the play or text and look at the places where your character speaks or others speak about him/her. Build your spidergram up gradually as you do so.

1 Use <u>white</u> <u>paper</u> <u>without</u> <u>lines</u> – it helps you think more clearly.

2 Use a pencil and a rubber – it is quicker and you can <u>add</u> <u>colours</u>, too.

3 Begin in the <u>middle</u> of the page with a title (this could be the name of a character or a theme) and put the <u>most</u> <u>important</u> <u>information</u> <u>around</u> <u>the</u> <u>title</u>.

4 Work your way out to the <u>margins</u> where you should put the <u>least</u> <u>important</u> <u>information</u>.

5 Your first five minutes are likely to be the <u>most</u> <u>productive</u> so do not stop for anything. You can make your map pretty and memorable afterwards.

6 Remember that the colours you choose for various topics of your spidergram can be <u>meaningful</u> because everything can be given an <u>appropriate</u> <u>colour</u>. Colours can also act as prompts to help you recall ideas.

7 You can make connections between ideas by <u>running</u> <u>branches</u> <u>off</u> <u>your</u> <u>main</u> <u>ideas</u>. Draw connecting branches to other main ideas if it seems sensible. Your spidergram will then take on the character of a colourful tube map; you can then add <u>appropriate</u> <u>pictures</u> <u>and</u> <u>images</u>.

8 Remember that pictures will bring ideas to life as well as help you remember them. If you are hopeless at drawing simply <u>cut</u> <u>likely</u> <u>pictures</u> <u>out</u> <u>of</u> <u>magazines</u>.

9 Keep spidergrams to <u>one</u> <u>piece</u> <u>of</u> <u>paper</u>. If you run out of space, tape another sheet of paper on to the side of the paper where you are running out of space. It does not matter how big your piece of paper is as long as it is <u>one</u> <u>side</u> <u>of</u> <u>paper</u>. You can always carefully fold it up afterwards. Boeing, the American aircraft corporation, uses this method to teach their engineers about their aircraft. The corporation has a huge 'quilted' spidergram that takes up the entire length of a hanger! The engineers learn the ins and outs of aircraft design in much less time than conventional methods: months rather than years!

Examiner's Top Tip
Try to get an overview of the themes of your particular play. Then see how a character relates to these themes.

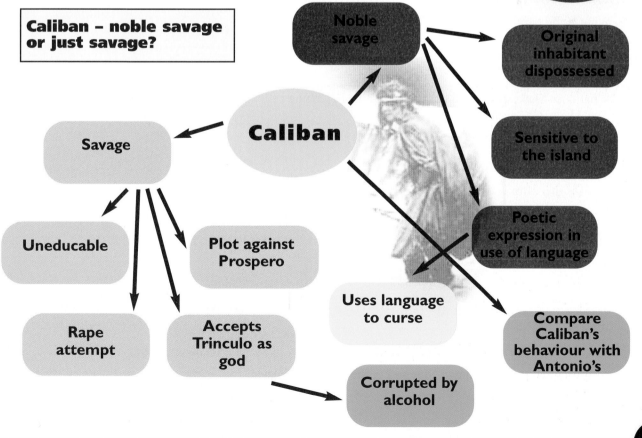

Caliban – noble savage or just savage?

- Noble savage
  - Original inhabitant dispossessed
  - Sensitive to the island
  - Poetic expression in use of language
  - Compare Caliban's behaviour with Antonio's
- Caliban
- Savage
  - Uneducable
  - Plot against Prospero
  - Rape attempt
  - Accepts Trinculo as god
    - Corrupted by alcohol
- Uses language to curse

EXAM QUESTIONS - Use the questions to test your progress. Check your answers on page 94–95.

The Shakespeare Assignment

1. Name two plays you may study.

....

2. Briefly explain a method of understanding passages from Shakespeare.

....

3. Identify two types of assignments that you could produce on a Shakespeare play.

....

4. What does 'textual evidence' mean?

....

5. Can the interpretation of a Shakespeare play change over time?

....

6. If so, why?

....

7. What does 'linguistic devices' mean?

....

8. What are the main genres of Shakespeare plays?

....

9. What does 'philosophical context' mean?

....

10. List the three styles of writing Shakespeare used in his plays.

....

11. Where did Shakespeare use poetic verse?

....

12. What is the purpose of blank verse?

....

Structure and Themes

13. What does Shakespeare like to establish at the beginning of his plays?

....

14. What happens next?

....

15. What is the 'climax' of a play?

....

16. What could happen during the 'climax' of a play?

....

17. Briefly explain what usually happens at the end of a Shakespeare play.

....

18. What is a 'theme'?

....

19. Identify three themes that can be found in Shakespeare's plays.

....

20. What type of themes might you expect to find in a comedy?

....

21. Briefly explain what is meant by 'dramatic contrast'.

....

22. Why did Shakespeare build dramatic contrasts into his plays?

....

23. Explain what is meant by 'self-knowledge'.

....

24. Briefly sum up the typical structure of a Shakespeare play.

....

Imagery and Essay Plans

25. What is meant by the term 'figures of speech'?

....

26. What is a simile?

....

27. Why is a metaphor a stronger comparison?

....

28. What is an extended metaphor?

....

29. What is meant by personification?

....

30. Define an oxymoron.

....

31. What is a motif?

....

32. Give two reasons why Shakespeare uses imagery in his plays.

....

33. Shakespeare uses a great deal of irony in his plays. What is irony?

....

34. What is dramatic irony?

....

35. Why and where would you expect to find passages rich in imagery?

....

36. Briefly sum up what is meant by imagery.

....

How did you do?

1–9	correct	start again
10–19	correct	getting there
20–29	correct	good work
30–36	correct	excellent

WHAT YOU HAVE TO STUDY

- <u>Poetry</u> is a significant part of the GCSE English and GCSE English Literature courses.

  In the AQA GCSE English course you are required to study one of two clusters of poetry from different cultures. This accounts for up to 15% of your final mark. The two clusters are of equal difficulty and the one that you study will probably depend on your teacher's personal preference.

- Most exam boards test your ability to read and understand poetry in your English Literature exams. In the AQA Literature specification you must compare two pre-1914 poems with two post-1914 poems. There are four post-1914 poets included in the AQA anthology but you will only study two of them. At present the pairs of poets are:

  Simon Armitage and Carol Ann Duffy

  Seamus Heaney and Gillian Clarke

  In the exam you will compare poems from either of these pairs with two poems taken from the pre-1914 poetry bank. This answer will account for 40% of your final marks.

  Other exam boards, such as Edexcel, have their own selections of poets or groups of poems under a specific <u>theme</u>.

- The type of poems that you will study will range from <u>ballads</u> (<u>narrative</u> or story poems) to <u>sonnets</u> (serious poems that explore deep themes, such as <u>love</u> and <u>death</u>) and you will be expected to make connections between them on the basis of content, theme and technique.

Examiner's Top Tip
Do not merely identify figures of speech and other poetic techniques, show how they affect meaning in your poem.

READING A POEM

Aim to read the poems at least <u>three times</u> and do the following very carefully.

- <u>Explain briefly what you think the poem is about.</u> You are looking for <u>an overview</u> at this stage. This early view of the poem may change once you have studied it in greater detail.

- <u>Examine how the poet gets their meaning across to us through their choice of form, language, imagery and themes.</u> You will also need to consider the poem's <u>tone</u>. For instance, what is the <u>attitude</u> of the <u>speaker</u> towards the topic or theme? What is their <u>attitude</u> to you? Does the poem's <u>tone</u> change in the poem? Go through each area as fully as you can.

- <u>Explain your views again on the poem,</u> stating what the poem is about. <u>Point out what can be learned</u> from the poem, including <u>any changes of mind</u> you may have had after working through the first two points given above.

Examiner's Top Tip
Try to write a poem of your own using a specific form. There is a lot to be learned about poetry by trying to write a poem of your own. You may even find that writing poetry gives you pleasure.

Chaucer SHELLEY WORDSWORTH t.s eliot coleridge Keats

HOW YOU WILL BE GRADED

To achieve grades C to A* you will need to:

- show that you have <u>engaged</u> with the poems by giving a <u>sustained</u> and <u>developed response</u> to <u>key words and phrases</u> in your essay question. More sophisticated answers will display <u>an enthusiastic personal response</u> with <u>close textual analysis</u>

- explore the poems and show <u>insight</u>. Again, more sophisticated responses will show <u>greater insight</u> or <u>exploration</u> of the poems

- <u>identify</u> the <u>verse form</u> and explain how its <u>genre</u> contributes towards the poem's <u>meaning</u>

- explain how the poet has used <u>language</u> and <u>imagery</u> in the poem. In other words, you will need to be able to identify word choices (<u>diction</u>) and what they may suggest as well as show how the poet uses <u>figures of speech</u>, such as <u>similes</u>, to <u>add meaning</u> to their <u>ideas</u> and <u>messages</u> in their poems. More developed responses will <u>show how the poet uses similar themes</u> or <u>points and ideas in several poems</u>. Such responses will also point out <u>similarities</u> or <u>contrasts</u> in the poet's use of <u>language, form</u> and other aspects of <u>poetic technique</u>

- say something about the poet's <u>purposes</u> and <u>intentions</u>. What is the poet setting out to achieve?

- identify with the <u>poet's intentions</u> or the <u>view of the narrator</u> in the poem. In other words, show <u>empathy</u>

- give a sophisticated response that is <u>convincing</u> and <u>imaginative, showing a high degree of empathy</u>

- display <u>analytical</u> and <u>interpretive</u> skills when examining the <u>social</u>, <u>moral</u> and <u>philosophical significance</u> of the poems.

HOW TO STUDY AND WRITE ABOUT POETRY (EN2)

QUICK TEST

1. How much of your final mark is your work on poetry likely to be worth?

2. What kind of poem is a ballad?

3. Where would you write your personal views in an exam essay?

4. How many times should you read a poem?

5. What is empathy?

5. Identifying with the theme or idea in a poem or perhaps the narrator's point of view
4. At least three times
3. At the end of your essay
2. A narrative poem
1. 15%

WRITING ABOUT POETRY (EN2)

TIPS ON WRITING ABOUT POETRY

One of the biggest problems in writing about poetry is finding <u>phrases</u> that enable you to <u>express</u> your <u>ideas</u> and make your writing <u>flow</u>. This <u>framework</u> is not really meant as a substitute for your structure, just a helping hand in case you get stuck. You should aim <u>to integrate useful phrases into your writing</u> so that you can explain yourself with ease in exams. Beware, however, of always using the same phrases, which would lead to a <u>mechanical style</u>.

- Introduce points that you want to make by using some of the phrases given below; change them around, or simply add them together. The more <u>fluent</u> you are the more <u>impressive</u> your points will be.

- Good grades in exams are achieved through <u>knowing your texts</u> and being able to <u>express</u> your points in a <u>fluent manner</u>. You will also be judged on your <u>punctuation</u>, your use of <u>standard English</u> and the <u>quality of your expression</u>.

- Look out for useful ways of <u>expressing</u> your <u>ideas</u> and making a note of them. Successful pupils are able to make their points in essays in a <u>fluent</u> and knowledgeable manner.

1. INTRODUCTORY PHRASES

- **The poem . . . is/seems to be about . . .**

- **The poem is narrated in the <u>first/second person</u>. This aids/enhances the poem's meaning as/because . . .**

- **The form of the poem is (a <u>ballad</u>/<u>sonnet</u>/<u>two-</u>, <u>three-</u>, <u>four-</u>, <u>five-line</u> <u>stanzas</u>/<u>free verse</u>) . . . This is an <u>appropriate</u> form for the poem because it helps readers <u>appreciate</u> . . .**

Examiner's Top Tip

Remember P.E.C. Point: make a point to address your question. Evidence: give a word, phrase or line of evidence for it. Comment: comment on your evidence and link it to the question.

2. PHRASES FOR THE MIDDLE OF A PIECE OF WRITING

- The theme/idea of . . . is present/repeated in both poems.
- For instance . . . . The poet contrasts . . . with . . . .
- The poet uses appropriate language/diction to convey a feeling of . . . . For instance . . .
- The caesura after . . . helps an audience understand . . . .
- The use of alliteration/assonance/onomatopoeia with . . . shows . . . .
- The poet's use of imagery (similes/metaphors/personification) can be seen with . . . . This shows/ intensifies the idea of . . . .
- Another interesting example of this is . . . . . This emphasises/shows/reinforces/gives a sense of/ refers to . . . .
- The poem's meaning is enhanced /deepened with . . .
- An example of which is . . . . This refers to the main idea of . . . .
- For example, this can be seen with . . . .
- The poem reflects the narrator's/poet's feelings on/of . . . .
- The poet reminds the reader of . . . with . . . .
- The poet draws attention to the fact that . . . .
- The poet compares . . . with . . . .

Examiner's Top Tip
It is important to be precise when writing about poetry. Remember that 'verse' means the whole poem or a collection of poems. You should use 'stanza' when you want to describe a part of a poem, such as a four-line 'quatrain'.

3. PHRASES TO SUM UP YOUR ARGUMENTS AND VIEWS

- *The poem's/narrator's tone is one of . . . . This helps the reader/audience appreciate the/how . . .*
- *The tone(s) in each poem is/are . . . . This/these show(s) . . .*
- *To sum up I would say that the poet feels . . . about his/her subject. The poet wants us to understand/feel the . . .*
- *Both/each of the poems show . . . . This shows the poet's feelings of . . .*
- *From reading these poems I learned that . . .*
- *My final view of the poem (s) is that it is /they are . . .*

QUICK TEST

1. What does P.E.C. mean?
2. Find out what the term 'caesura' means.
3. Find out the number of lines in a sonnet.
4. What is alliteration?
5. What is a writing frame?

5. A structured bank of phrases designed to help your writing flow
4. Repetition of consonants for an effect, for instance, the headline, 'Football Fever'
3. 14
2. A 'cut'. The term refers to any punctuation mark used in poetry.
1. Point – Evidence – Comment

COMPARING TWO OR MORE POEMS

FROM THE ENGLISH LITERARY HERITAGE (EN2)

THE ENGLISH LITERATURE EXAM

The English Literature exam asks you to write about four poems. You will have studied a pair of modern poets and you will need to compare two pre-1914 poems with two poems from the post-1914 poets you have studied. The pairs of modern poets are:

- **Carol Ann Duffy and Simon Armitage**
- **Seamus Heaney and Gillian Clarke**

In order to answer this question you will need to have a good idea of the characteristic themes, ideas and imagery used by your two modern poets and by the poets in the pre-1914 poetry bank.

THINGS TO LOOK OUT FOR IN CAROL ANN DUFFY'S POEMS

Carol Ann Duffy is interested in <u>characters</u>. *Havisham, Elvis's Twin Sister, Salome* and *Ann Hathaway* are all written about <u>characters</u> <u>from</u> <u>history</u> <u>or</u> <u>literature</u>. These poems express a variety of emotions from <u>love</u> (*Ann Hathaway*) to <u>bitterness</u> (*Havisham*). In *Education for Leisure* and *Stealing*, Carol Ann Duffy adopts the <u>persona</u> of two rather <u>unpleasant</u> <u>loners</u>.

Two of the poems are about <u>childhood</u> <u>memories</u>. *Before You Were Mine* seems to be <u>autobiographical</u>, whilst *We Remember Your Childhood Well* explores the darker side of <u>parent–child</u> <u>relationships</u>.

THINGS TO LOOK OUT FOR IN SIMON ARMITAGE'S POEMS

Simon Armitage is also interested in <u>characters</u>. In *Kid* he adopts the <u>persona</u> of Batman's sidekick Robin, whilst in *Those bastards…* and *Hitcher* he imagines himself as rather <u>less</u> <u>socially</u> <u>responsible</u> <u>characters</u>. *Mother any distance…, My father thought it…, Homecoming* and *November* all deal with <u>parent–child</u> <u>relationships</u> and may be <u>autobiographical</u>. In *I've made out a will…* Simon Armitage faces up to his own <u>death</u> in a light-hearted fashion, whereas a character in *November* faces up to the <u>death</u> <u>of</u> <u>a</u> <u>close</u> <u>relative</u>.

THINGS TO LOOK OUT FOR IN SEAMUS HEANEY'S POEMS

Many of Seamus Heaney's poems seem to be <u>autobiographical</u>. *Blackberry-Picking, Death of a Naturalist* and *Mid-Term Break* relate incidents from his <u>childhood</u> including the <u>death</u> <u>of</u> <u>a</u> <u>close</u> <u>relative</u> (*Mid-Term Break*). *Digging* and *Follower* concern his <u>relationship</u> <u>with</u> <u>his</u> <u>father</u>. *Storm on the Island, Perch* and *At a Potato Digging* describe various aspects of <u>life</u> <u>in</u> <u>rural</u> <u>Ireland</u>. Almost all of Heaney's poems concern some aspect of <u>nature</u>.

THINGS TO LOOK OUT FOR IN GILLIAN CLARKE'S POEMS

Gillian Clarke also discusses <u>rural</u> <u>life</u> and <u>nature</u> in *A Difficult Birth, Easter 1998* and *The Field-Mouse* but she adds a <u>political</u> dimension to these two poems. *Catrin, Baby-sitting Mali* and *Cold Knap Lake* discuss <u>adult</u> <u>and</u> <u>child</u> <u>relationships</u> and appear to be <u>autobiographical</u> as do *A Difficult Birth*, *Easter 1998*, *October* (about <u>death</u> and <u>growing</u> <u>old</u>) and *On the Train*.

THINGS TO LOOK OUT FOR IN THE PRE-1914 POETRY BANK

On My First Sonne is an <u>autobiographical</u> poem about the <u>death</u> <u>of</u> a <u>close</u> <u>relative</u>.
The Song of the Old Mother is about <u>growing</u> <u>old</u> and <u>adult</u> <u>and</u> <u>child</u> <u>relationships</u>.
The Afflictions of Margaret is told about <u>adult</u> <u>and</u> <u>child</u> <u>relationships</u>.
The Little Boy Lost / The Little Boy Found is about <u>adult</u> <u>and</u> <u>child</u> <u>relationships</u>.
Tichborne's Elegy is an <u>autobiographical</u> poem about <u>death</u>.
The Man He Killed is about <u>death</u> in war.
Patrolling Barnegat is a description of <u>nature</u>.
Sonnet 130 is about <u>love</u>.
My Last Duchess is about <u>love</u>, pride and <u>murder</u>. It is uses the <u>persona</u> of a <u>character</u> <u>from</u> <u>history</u>.
The Laboratory is about <u>love</u>, jealousy and <u>murder</u>. It uses the <u>persona</u> of a <u>character</u> <u>from</u> <u>history</u>.
Ulysses is about facing up to <u>old</u> age and <u>death</u>. It uses the <u>persona</u> of a <u>character</u> <u>from</u> <u>literature</u>.
The Village Schoolmaster is a study in <u>character</u>. It has a <u>political</u> message.
The Eagle is a study of a creature in <u>nature</u>.
Inversnaid attempts to describe a <u>natural</u> landscape.
Sonnet expressed the poet's enthusiasm for <u>nature</u>.

ANSWERING A QUESTION

For your <u>exam</u> <u>question</u> you will normally be asked to <u>compare</u> <u>a</u> <u>named</u> <u>poem</u> <u>with</u> <u>three</u> <u>others</u> <u>of</u> <u>your</u> <u>choice</u>. You must compare <u>one</u> <u>poem</u> by each of the <u>modern</u> <u>authors</u> you have studied with <u>two</u> <u>poems</u> taken from the <u>pre-1914</u> <u>poetry</u> <u>bank</u>.

If you have studied Seamus Heaney and Gillian Clarke, you might be asked the following question:

> Compare the ways that poets use nature in 4 or more of the poems you have studied, including at least one by each poet. You should write about '*A Difficult Birth*' by Gillian Clarke, and compare it with at least one poem by Seamus Heaney and 2 poems from the Pre-1914 Poetry Bank

If you have studied Simon Armitage and Carol Ann Duffy, you might be asked:

> Compare at least 4 poems from those you have studied where strong dislike for another person is shown. Write about '*My Last Duchess*' by Robert Browning, one poem by Carol Ann Duffy, one poem by Simon Armitage, and one other poem from the Pre-1914 Poetry Bank.
> Compare:
> * the reasons for dislike in the poems
> * how the poets convey dislike.

The first thing to do in answering these questions is <u>to</u> <u>look</u> <u>at</u> <u>the</u> <u>named</u> <u>poem</u>. Try to decide <u>how</u> <u>the</u> <u>key</u> <u>idea</u> <u>from</u> <u>the</u> <u>question</u> <u>is</u> <u>handled</u> and <u>think</u> <u>of</u> <u>other</u> <u>similar</u> poems. Fortunately, although there are a large number of poems, they revolve around <u>a</u> <u>limited</u> <u>number</u> <u>of</u> <u>themes</u> <u>and</u> <u>techniques</u>.

PLANNING AN ESSAY ON POEMS

FROM THE ENGLISH LITERARY HERITAGE (EN2)

You will need to **plan your essay carefully** based on the poems you have chosen and the **key words** you have identified in the question. It's a good idea to **make a table to help you** to make **comparisons**. The table below refers to the question on 'use of nature' on the previous page.

Use of nature	Themes	How theme is shown	Use of language and imagery	Verse form, rhyme etc.
A Difficult Birth				
Storm on the Island				
Patrolling Barnegat				
Inversnaid				

This table is not to scale. You can use a whole page of your exam booklet if you wish.

ORGANISING YOUR ESSAY

You will need to think carefully about how you organise your comparison of four poems.

- If you have chosen **four quite similar poems,** the order is not very important.
- If you have chosen **pairs of poems in sharp contrast**, discuss one pair and then the other.
- **Four poems can be arranged into a continuum** – work your way from 'best' to 'worst' or from 'worst' to 'best'.

Care over the order of your discussion will help you to avoid repetition and should give it some logical flow.

PLANNING YOUR ESSAY

If you use a large table to make notes, you should be able to fill it in with details and references to the poems. Alternatively, you could use a spidergram.

Once you have decided on what you wish to say, you could structure your essay along the following lines:

INTRODUCTION

WHAT POEM 1 HAS TO SAY ON THE TOPIC. How it works. Some similarities and differences between poem 1 and the other poems.	**WHAT POEM 3 HAS TO SAY ON THE TOPIC.** How it works. Some similarities and differences between poem 3 and the other poems.
WHAT POEM 2 HAS TO SAY ON THE TOPIC. How it works. Some similarities and differences between poem 2 and the other poems.	**WHAT POEM 4 HAS TO SAY ON THE TOPIC.** How it works. Some similarities and differences between poem 4 and the other poems.

A second way of comparing the poems is to decide on your areas of interest and work through each poem's contribution to that area. For instance, you can use significant points, such as major areas of agreement or disagreement.

STARTING YOUR ESSAY

Begin your essay by stating how all four of the poems relate to the topic. You could start the nature essay in the following way:

> A Difficult Birth, Storm on the Island, Patrolling Barnegat and Inversnaid all make use of nature but the four poets show very different attitudes to it. In A Difficult Birth, Gillian Clarke describes a very natural scene but she uses this scene to comment on politics. Storm on the Island also describes nature but Seamus Heaney is more interested in human concerns than the natural events in the poem. Walt Whitman, on the other hand, seems genuinely interested in giving an account of a storm – people appear only dimly at the end. Of the four poems only Inversnaid attempts to evoke a natural landscape with no people at all.

In this example the poems have been sorted into a continuum to allow comparisons between their different aspects.

Examiner's Top Tip
This question needs a great deal of planning – do not try to do it all in the exam. Revise possible essay plans as well as the poems.

A FOUR-WAY COMPARISON

In the body of your essay you need to manage comparisons across four poems. This will mean that you will sometimes need to make statements about all four poems in a single paragraph. In an essay on the poets' use of <u>characters from history and fiction</u>, for instance, you might say:

> Simon Armitage chooses a character from popular comic books, TV and film in Kid. Most readers will recognise Robin from the *Batman* films and this is not a barrier to understanding Armitage's discussion of old age. Carol Ann Duffy invents a character in Elvis's Twin Sister but she is so close to Elvis Presley that the points she wants to make about fame are easily made. However, some of her points might be lost if the reader does not know the words to *Heartbreak Hotel*. Tennyson's use of Ulysses was an obvious one in the 19th century as most people studied Latin and Greek stories at school. It is less likely that modern readers will be familiar with Ulysses' adventures, but Tennyson mentions enough of them in the poem for us to understand what he is saying about facing up to old age and death. The odd one out in this group is My Last Duchess. It seems there was a historical character who acted like the Duke but he is so obscure that very few people have heard of him. Browning therefore provides all we need to know about the Duke in the poem itself. He doesn't get the benefit of the reader's prior knowledge in the same way as the others.

You can see that it takes a long time to consider four poems and you will need to practise writing this style of essay well in advance. Notice how the above answer says that three poems are similar and that one is different. Usually these similarities and differences will shift depending on which point you are making.

WRITING ESSAYS ON POEMS

FROM THE ENGLISH LITERARY HERITAGE (EN2)

WHAT TO SAY IN YOUR ESSAY

There are two main ways in which you might be asked to compare the poems:
- by content – this will include subject, theme and setting
- by technique – this will include imagery and poetic forms, such as the dramatic monologue or the sonnet.

Content comparisons are discussed in the section on Texts From Different Cultures (page 75). The 'content' might also consist of people's reactions, as in a question that asks you to discuss 'poems that some people might find disturbing'. Remember, however, that this is a literature exam and, even in content comparisons, you should try to include some discussion of technique.

DISCUSSING POETIC TECHNIQUE

The poems from the pre-1914 poetry bank tend to be more formal in their use of things like figurative language, specific verse forms and rhyme schemes but there are techniques that stretch across at least four poems in the collection. For instance, <u>sonnets</u> are used by Simon Armitage (*Those bastards…, I've made a will…*), Carol Ann Duffy (*Ann Hathaway*), Shakespeare (*Sonnet 130*) and John Clare (*Sonnet*). <u>Dramatic</u> <u>monologues</u> are used by Simon Armitage (*Kid, Hitcher*), Carol Ann Duffy (*Stealing, Education for Leisure*), Robert Browning (*My Last Duchess, The Laboratory*) and Alfred Tennyson (*Ulysses*). More generally, you might be asked to comment on almost any poet's <u>use of imagery</u> or <u>choice of language</u>.

For a poetic form (sonnet, dramatic monologue) essay you need to:
- have a good grasp of the rules of the from, e.g. rhyme scheme, use of persona
- be able to discuss how each poem uses the form
- be able to discuss how the poets adapt the form for their own purposes
- be able to assess the effectiveness of the use of the form

A POSSIBLE APPROACH

Four poems that use dramatic monologues are:
Simon Armitage's *Hitcher*, Carol Ann Duffy's *Education for Leisure*, Robert Browning's *My Last Duchess* and *The Laboratory*.
Interestingly, all four poems could be classed as 'disturbing' as they all concern murder.

Dramatic monologue – a poem in the first person in which the poet adopts a persona and addresses an unspeaking implied listener. Often written in the present tense, as in a speech made on stage.

HITCHER

This poem is about a motorist who picks up a hitchhiker. The motorist finds the contrast between his humdrum existence and the hitcher's carefree life so annoying that he hits the hitchhiker across the head with his Krooklok and then dumps him out of the car in an isolated place. The poem uses some aspects of the dramatic monologue, e.g. the use of a persona, but it is told in the past tense and there is no implied listener.

EDUCATION FOR LEISURE

This poem concerns a speaker who is so bored by his own existence that he has taken to killing as a way of making himself feel important. He has killed several small animals but at the end of the poem, he goes out to kill a person. This turns out to be the reader. The poem is in the present tense and good use is made of the idea of an implied listener.

MY LAST DUCHESS

This poem is spoken by a Renaissance Duke who had his last wife killed for being too easily pleased and not appreciating his aristocratic heritage. The implied listener is an ambassador who has come to arrange his next marriage.

The poem makes good use of a dramatic situation – the two men are looking at a portrait of the Duchess, and the persona is interestingly cruel. There is an interesting use of run-on lines and rhyme.

THE LABORATORY

This poem is spoken by an aristocratic French woman from about the time of Louis XIV. Her lover has betrayed her with another woman. She has gone to a laboratory to purchase poison with which to poison her rival. The implied listener is the chemist. There is an interesting use of rhythm to establish relatively light tone.

In writing this essay it would be a good idea to discuss the two poems by Browning first. In this way, you can establish your understanding of 'classic' dramatic monologues first. It will also allow you to discuss Duffy's interesting use of the implied listener at the end of her poem. Finally, you can discuss whether Armitage's poem has enough features of a classic dramatic monologue to count as one at all. You could then go on to discuss how well each poet explores the personality of the persona they have adopted.

DISCUSSING IMAGERY AND LANGUAGE

For imagery and language essays you need to:
- choose a set of poems that use imagery or language in broadly similar ways
- make comparisons of similar images or language choices
- be able to discuss any contrasts between the different poems
- be able to assess how well the poet uses imagery or language.

This type of response can be very open-ended and you need to choose poems that are 'rich' enough in language to provide material for you to discuss.

Some interesting features you might like to explore are:
- Simon Armitage's use of domestic imagery in *Mother any distance...*
- Carol Ann Duffy's use of Elvis Presley songs in *Elvis's Twin Sister*
- Seamus Heaney's use of military imagery at the end of *Death of a Naturalist*
- Gillian Clarke's use of natural imagery in *November*
- Shakespeare's criticism of the imagery used in love poetry in *Sonnet 130*
- Walt Whitman's use of verb forms in *Patrolling Barnegat*
- Gerard Manley Hopkin's use of dialect words and alliteration in *Inversnaid*.

Balance

You may find some poems easier to discuss than others but it is important to keep your discussion as balanced as possible. Write approximately the same amount on each poem.

TEXTS FROM DIFFERENT CULTURES (EN2)
English from around the world

WHAT YOU MAY STUDY

You will either study a number of <u>poems</u>, *or* <u>short</u> <u>stories</u> *or* <u>novels</u> *written by English speakers from different countries around the world. Whether you write about these texts for coursework or for your final exams depends upon the* <u>specification</u> *of the exam board that your school is following. Whatever you study, you will need to adopt the same approach. In your course-work or exam answers you will need to:*

- *show that you* <u>understand</u> *what you have read and* <u>know</u> <u>how</u> <u>it</u> <u>relates</u> *to other texts in 'Different Cultures'*

- *display an* <u>awareness</u> *of the* <u>themes</u> <u>and</u> <u>ideas</u> *in the texts which make them* <u>distinctive</u>

- *make* <u>comparisons</u> *between the texts in your essays. The current AQA Anthology provides two clusters of poems from different cultures. You will need to study only one of these clusters.*

FINDING LINKS BETWEEN THE POEMS

Look for <u>common</u> <u>ideas</u> or <u>themes</u> that can help you make <u>links</u> between the stories or poems you study. Among such <u>ideas</u> and <u>themes</u> try to find:

feelings about being <u>caught</u> <u>between</u> two <u>cultures</u>

feelings about <u>change</u> <u>or how</u> things <u>do</u> <u>not</u> change

ideas about <u>language</u> and <u>identity</u>

ideas about <u>language, power</u> and <u>dialect</u>

feelings about <u>independence</u>

<u>beliefs</u> <u>and</u> <u>ritual</u>

<u>protest</u> <u>against</u> <u>ideas</u> <u>and</u> <u>attitudes</u> (this will include <u>racism</u>)

differences in <u>attitudes</u> <u>and</u> <u>values</u>

<u>customs</u> <u>and</u> <u>traditions</u>

HOW YOU WILL BE GRADED

To achieve grades C to A* or higher you will need to <u>compare</u> the texts. As you do so you should:

- show an <u>understanding</u> of the texts' <u>main</u> <u>characters</u>

- give a <u>sustained</u> and <u>developed</u> knowledge of the texts and show an <u>awareness</u> of the writers' <u>purposes</u>

- show <u>insight</u> and the <u>ability</u> to <u>explore</u> these texts

- reveal <u>a</u> <u>structured</u> <u>understanding</u> of how <u>thoughts</u> <u>and</u> <u>feelings</u> are revealed in the texts

- <u>display</u> <u>an</u> <u>awareness</u> of how <u>form</u>, <u>language</u> and <u>imagery</u> are used and <u>comment</u> on how these contribute towards <u>meaning</u> in the texts

- make <u>effective</u> <u>use</u> of <u>textual</u> <u>detail</u> to <u>support</u> <u>your</u> <u>arguments</u>. At higher levels reveal <u>a</u> <u>convincing</u> and <u>imaginative</u> <u>interpretation</u> of the texts

- show involvement through <u>personal</u> <u>empathy</u>. That is, <u>appreciate</u> the writer's <u>concerns</u>, <u>ideas</u> or <u>attitudes</u>. At the higher levels you will exhibit <u>a</u> <u>high</u> <u>degree</u> <u>of</u> <u>empathy</u>

- place people and powerful <u>emotions</u> in the context of <u>local</u> <u>customs</u> and <u>traditions</u>.

- engage with texts by showing <u>an</u> <u>enthusiastic</u> <u>personal</u> <u>response</u>.

SOME ESSENTIAL POETIC TERMS

USE OF LETTER AND WORD SOUNDS

- Alliteration: the same consonant at the beginning of words repeated for an effect: 'fireside flickers'.
- Assonance: repetition of vowel sounds for an effect: 'icy winds knife us'. The repetition of the vowel 'i' helps stress the coldness of the 'winds'.
- Onomatopoeia: words which sound like their meaning: 'buzz' and 'click'.
- Rhythm and rhyme: the poem's pace when read aloud and word endings that sound alike for an effect.

IMAGERY

- Metaphor: a stronger comparison where 'is' or 'are' is used or implied: 'Juliet is the sun.'
- Personification: ('person-making'): giving an animal, idea or noun human feelings to enhance an emotion, feeling or effect: 'Arise fair sun and kill the envious moon.'
- Oxymoron: figures of speech in which contradictory, opposite words are yoked together for an effect. For example, The Beatles, the great 1960s' pop band, famously had a hit song and a film entitled A Hard Day's Night.
  Oxymorons can also be paradoxes to enliven prose but some have turned into clichés: 'act naturally', 'living dead', etc.
- Simile: a comparison using 'as' or 'like': 'My love is as deep as the sea.'

PUNCTUATION AND FORM

- Ballad: a story poem that usually features dramatic stories about ordinary people.
- Couplet: a two-line stanza that rhymes.
- Caesura or cesura: means 'a cutting'. It can be any type of punctuation in poetry that causes the reader to pause. Poets use them to end-stop their lines and to emphasise points and ideas in their poetry. A caesura can add a great deal of meaning if placed in the middle of a line.
- Elegy: a poem for a dead person.
- Enjambment or run-on line/run-on stanza: one line runs into another to achieve a poetic effect, often used to aid rhythm and help enact something.

- Free verse: irregular stanzas, filled with lines of varying length. The lines are like waves coming in along a sea-shore: each has natural rhythm and is just long enough. The form suits conversational and argumentative poems. Free verse, or vers libre, was the most popular form of poetry in the twentieth century and still remains so.
- Lyric: a poem that sets out the thoughts and feelings of a single speaker.
- Quatrain: four lines of a poem that rhyme. It is the main unit in English poetry.
- Stanza: a clear section of a poem, usually two or four lines.
- Sonnet: usually a 14-line poem about a serious theme such as love or death.
- Triplet or Tercet: a three-line stanza; this is a form suited for comic poetry, but watch out for when poets reverse the expected content, as with Seamus Heaney's Mid-Term Break. The effect can be very poignant.
- Verse: an entire poem or collection of poems or poetry.

NARRATIVE STANCE AND ATTITUDES WITHIN POEMS

- Narrator (first and third person): if the whole poem is spoken by the first-person narrator, who is clearly not the poet, then this is known as a dramatic monologue. For an example, read Robert Browning's poem My Last Duchess.
- Tone: a poet's or narrator's attitude towards their subject and audience. Note that tone can change within a poem to emphasise changes of meaning. The poet's use of diction (words deliberately chosen for their associations and sounds) can affect the tone of a poem. For example, contrasts between multi-syllable and one-syllable words can very quickly change the mood of a poem. In Carol Ann Duffy's poem Education for Leisure, the contrast between the fizzy polysyllabic 'pavements suddenly glitter' and the monosyllabic 'I touch your arm' is very chilling indeed.

QUICK TEST

1. What is a simile?

2. Explain what empathy means.

3. Give an example of onomatopoeia.

4. What is the difference between 'verse' and a 'stanza'?

5. What is a suitable subject for a sonnet and why?

Examiner's Top Tip
It is not enough simply to identify poetic terms – you have got to show how they add meaning to a poem.

5. 'Love' or 'death' because sonnets usually have serious subject matter
4. 'Verse' is an entire poem or collection of poems; a 'stanza' is a section of a poem.
3. Buzz (or any word that sounds like its meaning)
2. An appreciation of a writer's or narrator's concerns and ideas
1. A comparison using 'as' or 'like'

Half-Caste

5.

1.

Excuse me
standing on one leg
I'm half-caste

Explain yuself
what yu mean
when yu say half-caste
yu mean when picasso
mix red an green
is a half-caste canvas
explain yuself
wha yu mean
when yu say half-caste
yu mean when light an shadow
mix in de sky
is a half-caste weather
well in dat case
england weather
nearly always half-caste
in fact some o dem cloud
half-caste till dem overcast
so spiteful dem dont want de sun pass
ah rass
explain yuself
wha yu mean
when yu say half-caste
yu mean tchaikovsky
sit down at dah piano
an mix a black key
wid a white key
is a half-caste symphony

Explain yuself
wha yu mean
Ah listening to yu wid de keen
half of mih ear
Ah lookin at yu wid de keen
half of mih eye
and when I'm introduced to yu

I'm sure you'll understand
why I offer yu half-a-hand
an when I sleep at night
I close half-a-eye
consequently when I dream
I dream half-a-dream
an when moon begin to glow
I half-caste human being
cast half-a-shadow
but yu must come back tomorrow
wid de whole of yu eye
an de whole of yu ear
an de whole of yu mind

6.

an I will tell yu
de other half
of my story

John Agard

Unrelated Incidents

this is thi
six a clock
news thi
man said n
thi reason
a talk wia
BBC accent
iz coz yi
widny wahnt
mi ti talk
aboot thi
trooth wia
voice lik
wanna yoo
scruff. if
a toktaboot
thi trooth
lik wanna yoo
scruff yi
widny thingk
it wuz troo.
jist wanna yoo
scruff tokn.
thirza right
way ti spell
ana right way
ti tok it. this
is me tokn yir
right way a
spellin. this
is ma trooth.
yooz doant no
thi trooth
yirsellz cawz
yi canny talk
right. this is
the six a clock
nyooz. belt up.

2.

3.

4.

Tom Leonard

```
Important Point
```
In an exam you will be unlikely to write as much as this. You
will also need to give more brief quotations to support your
points than are given above. Even so, a few points made well
with appropriately chosen evidence would
secure you a good mark.

```
INTERNET
```
Useful exercises and ideas about 'Poems And
Texts from Different Cultures' and help with other
exam poetry and texts can be found at:
www.englishresources.co.uk

WHAT THE POEMS ARE ABOUT

1. Both poems deal with issues of <u>language</u>, <u>power</u> and <u>prejudice</u>.

2. Leonard <u>ironically</u> reverses the usual <u>dialects</u> associated with <u>authority</u> and reading the news (<u>received pronunciation</u> and <u>standard</u> <u>English)</u>. He wants us to think about issues of <u>truth</u> and <u>authority</u> when we only hear the news read by people with <u>received pronunciation</u> or <u>standard</u> <u>English</u>.

3. He argues that it is wrong and prejudiced to believe that these <u>dialects</u> are the only ones capable of expressing the truth and so be taken seriously. His angry <u>narrator</u> shows that such prejudice is silly and wrong, especially as <u>the narrator</u> <u>argues</u> <u>that</u> <u>his</u> working-class Glaswegian <u>dialect</u> <u>is</u> <u>the</u> <u>only</u> <u>one</u> <u>which</u> <u>should</u> <u>be</u> <u>taken</u> <u>seriously;</u> it is as if the local dialect is a cut above anyone else's because it is the only one capable of expressing the 'trooth'. Leonard infers that <u>'trooth'</u> <u>can</u> <u>be</u> <u>told</u> <u>in</u> <u>any</u> <u>dialect</u>.

4. The <u>tone</u> of his poem <u>is</u> <u>one</u> <u>of</u> <u>anger</u> <u>against</u> <u>the</u> <u>prejudices</u> <u>of</u> <u>society</u> where working-class dialects are not taken seriously and given no respect. Leonard thinks that speakers of <u>local</u> <u>dialects</u> are not given the consideration and status that they deserve.

5. Agard's <u>narrator</u> eloquently shows, through a number of unusual and convincing <u>comparisons,</u> that it is wrong to label anyone by using the term 'half-caste'. The unquestioned use of such terms can lead to the prejudice of seeing someone as only <u>half a person</u>.

6. Agard and Leonard show us that <u>power, authority and prejudice are linked with language and how we use it</u>. They warn us against blindly accepting some dialects, such as standard <u>English</u>, as voices of <u>authority</u> and <u>correctness</u> while excluding others and their speakers as only worthy of ridicule. <u>The</u> <u>'truth'</u> <u>can</u> <u>be</u> <u>expressed</u> <u>in</u> <u>other</u> <u>dialects</u> <u>too</u>.

HOW TO COMPARE TEXTS FROM DIFFERENT CULTURES (EN2)

You have to write a comparative essay comparing two or more texts. On these pages there are examples of what you should try to achieve. Your first aim in exams is to write about poems that are naturally linked through themes, ideas, or layout. See the previous pages for suggestions on linking the poems or texts.

• Write about the importance of language and form in *Half-Caste* (by John Agard) and *Unrelated Incidents* (by Tom Leonard).

HOW MEANING IN THE POEMS IS EXPRESSED

• **The impact of each poem's argument is enhanced through being spoken by a <u>first-person</u> <u>narrator</u>. Both are appropriately set out in <u>free</u> <u>verse</u>, in which the dialect is defiantly proclaimed and <u>phonetically</u> spelled in <u>lines of</u> <u>varying</u> <u>length</u>. The narrowness of the poems' lines contrast with other poems written in <u>standard</u> <u>English</u>. The poets may intend the form of their poems to act as a badge for the dignity, independence and truthfulness of their dialects. The form of each poem is thus appropriate for the arguments and language deployed by the poets.**

• **The rules of <u>standard</u> <u>English</u> have no place in these poems as there is no punctuation, nor capital letters. The <u>narrators</u> make their points with <u>questions, arguments</u> <u>and</u> <u>statements</u>. The idea is to advance <u>an alternative</u> <u>to standard English.</u> Agard's poem has <u>stanzas</u> in which some of the <u>senses</u> are alluded to. Leonard's poem is plainer, using a single stanza or <u>verse paragraph</u> to refer to speech and <u>Glaswegian</u> <u>dialect</u>. The poets may be from different parts of the world yet there is a similarity in their views on language about <u>what</u> should be said and <u>how</u> it should be expressed.**

• **Both poems have <u>an</u> <u>ironic</u> <u>tone</u> intended to startle their audiences into accepting the truth of the arguments that they advance. Phrases such as 'belt up' and 'ah rass' disclose their respective <u>tones</u>.**

Examiner's Top Tip
You only have half an hour in your exam. Make a few points well. Give evidence for each point and comment on it. You cannot say everything!

Try to tie the main comparative points of the poems together briefly and give your views.

EXAM QUESTIONS - Use the questions to test your progress. Check your answers on page 95.

How to Read and Study Poetry

1. How many poems do you have to write about in your Literature exam?
....

2. Are you being tested on your reading or your writing?
....

3. Name two forms for poems.
....

4. How many times should you read your poems?
....

5. What is tone?
....

6. What are the main forms of narration?
....

7. Diction is another word for the word choices that poets make for their poems. True or false?
....

8. What is a theme?
....

9. Part of a poem is a verse. True or false?
....

10. Which other post-1914 poet will you study if you are reading Simon Armitage?
....

11. The classroom 'glowed like a sweet shop' is a metaphor. True or false?
....

12. Name the post-1914 poet that is paired with Gillian Clarke.
....

How to Write About Poems

13. How many poems do you need to compare in your final English exam?
....

14. What is enjambment?
....

15. What does it mean to 'compare and contrast' when writing about poetry?
....

16. What is an oxymoron?
....

17. What can an oxymoron suggest?
....

18. Quatrains are the main units of English poetry. True or false?
....

19. What is free verse?
....

20. Why is free verse appropriate for certain poems?
....

21. What is assonance?

....

22. Where should you give your personal view of the poems that you write about?

....

Texts from Different Cultures

23. What are 'Texts from Different Cultures'?

....

24. What form is most favoured by poets from 'Different Cultures'?

....

25. Identify two dialects spoken by poets from other cultures.

....

26. Name three texts by writers or poets of 'Different Cultures' from the exam syllabus that you are following.

....

27. Give three themes or ideas that can be explored in these texts.

....

28. Once you identify a figure of speech or some other poetic technique what must you do afterwards?

....

29. John Agard uses no caesuras in his poem. True or false?

....

30. The narrow lines of Tom Leonard and John Agard's poems suit the dialect that they use. True or false?

....

31. Why do Tom Leonard and John Agard use free verse?

....

32. In his poem Half-Caste, John Agard argues that the unthinking use of the standard English phrase 'half-caste' leads to negative implications. What are these implications?

....

33. How long do you have to plan and write your essay in the final exam?

....

34. Identify two poems from 'Different Cultures' in the AQA Anthology that are connected by the theme of change. If you are studying with another exam board identify a theme that is present in two or more texts.

....

35. How many clusters of poems from 'Different Cultures' are there in the AQA Anthology?

....

36. How many clusters do you study?

....

How did you do?

1–9	correct	start again
10–19	correct	getting there
20–29	correct	good work
30–36	correct	excellent

STUDYING NOVELS AND SHORT STORIES (EN2)

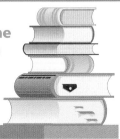

Novels and short stories are studied as part of the English and English Literature specifications. For the AQA English exam you must study one prose text by an author on the exam board's lists. If you study English and English Literature, the text you study for coursework must be a pre-1914 text, whilst the text you study for the exam must be one of the texts set by the board.

In summary, this means:

English only
  • 1 novel or collection of stories — can be pre- or post-1914 — coursework assessed.

English and English Literature
  • 1 novel or collection of stories — pre-1914 — coursework assessed in English and in English Literature.
  • 1 novel or collection of stories — post-1914 — exam.

To **gain** **the** **higher** **grades** you will need to **demonstrate** **knowledge** of the **social**, **historical** **or** **cultural** **setting** of the novel or collection of short stories.

Points to Remember

  • The coursework prose study specifies authors and not titles. You may be able to study a book of your own choice.
  • If you choose a collection of short stories, they should be about as demanding as a novel in terms of complexity, range and sustained reading.
  • A post-1914 text must be written by an author with a well established critical reputation, and must be worthy of serious study.
  • This piece of coursework can be assessed orally.
  • Your language and style will affect the impression you create even when they are not being directly assessed.
  • Topic sentences introduce points and hold your work together.

Examiner's Top Tip
The term 'text' can refer to any form of writing and you should refer to your books, stories or poems as texts in your writing.

HOW YOU WILL BE GRADED

You will be assessed on your ability to read and show your understanding through writing or speaking about your chosen texts.

To achieve C to A* you should aim to:
• show insight into the <u>implications</u> and <u>relevance</u> of a text
• comment on its <u>style</u>, <u>structure</u> and <u>characters</u>
• discuss the <u>writer's</u> <u>use</u> <u>of</u> <u>language</u>.

To get a grade A or better you will need to show <u>analytical</u> and <u>interpretative</u> skills when evaluating:
• the <u>moral</u>, <u>philosophical</u> and <u>social</u> <u>significance</u> of a text
• <u>significant</u> <u>achievements</u> within the <u>prose-fiction</u> <u>genre</u>
• the <u>writer's</u> <u>narrative</u> <u>craft</u> and appeal to the <u>reader</u>
• <u>patterns</u> <u>and</u> <u>details</u> <u>of</u> <u>language</u> exploited for implication or suggestion.

POSSIBLE ASSIGNMENTS

Assignments that are assessed for both English and English Literature exams are known as 'cross-over' assignments.

These might include the following.

- A <u>close</u> <u>analysis</u> <u>of</u> <u>a</u> <u>chapter</u> of a novel. You would need to show its significance to the text as a whole and show awareness of the novel's <u>historical</u> <u>or</u> <u>social</u> <u>context</u>. For example, a study of the opening chapter of *Great Expectations* by Charles Dickens.
- An exploration of an author's <u>approach</u> <u>to</u> <u>a</u> <u>character</u> <u>or</u> <u>theme</u> in a novel or range of short stories. You would need to note the <u>effects</u> <u>of</u> <u>social,</u> <u>historical or cultural influences</u>. For example, Charlotte Bronte's exploration of the role of women in *Jane Eyre*.
- An <u>examination</u> <u>of</u> <u>a</u> <u>particular</u> <u>genre</u>, such as <u>science</u> <u>fiction</u> or <u>detective</u> <u>stories</u>. You would need to study a range of stories and show a knowledge of literary tradition as well as <u>social,</u> <u>historical or cultural context</u>. For example, a study of the role of the scientist in the stories of H G Wells.
- A comparison of the way an <u>issue</u> <u>or</u> <u>theme</u>, such as relationships between men and women, is treated in a range of short stories, showing awareness of cultural contexts. For example, a study of relationships in the short stories of Thomas Hardy.
- An investigation of an <u>author's</u> <u>use</u> <u>of</u> <u>settings</u> in the novel or group of short stories, showing knowledge of literary contexts. For instance, moor and valley in Emily Bronte's *Wuthering Heights*.
- A structured interview with the teacher about your response to and understanding of key features of a text, the <u>author's</u> <u>choice</u> <u>of</u> <u>language</u> and structure, and the <u>social,</u> <u>historical</u> <u>and</u> <u>cultural</u> <u>context</u> <u>of</u> <u>the</u> <u>text</u>. For instance, a structured interview on Mary Shelley's *Frankenstein*.

If you are entering two coursework prose study assignments, one for English Literature and one for English, you have a wider choice of texts. These might include:

- A study of five or six short stories in the same genre, written by different authors and published before 1914, showing awareness of social, historical and cultural contexts. For instance, a comparative study of stories by Poe and Maupassant (in translation).
- An analysis of technique in a novel by an author not included on the National Curriculum list, such as Bram Stoker's *Dracula*, showing awareness of literary tradition and social, historical and cultural contexts.

If you are studying English but not English Literature, you could consider:

- a study of William Golding's use of symbolism in *Lord of the Flies*
- an analysis of the importance of one or more characters in a novel
- a study of a writer's technique across a range of short stories.

QUICK TEST

1. How many novels do you have to study if you are taking the English and English Literature option?

2. How many do you have to study if you are taking the English and English Literature option and wish to write about a novel that is not on the National Curriculum list?

3. What is the historical context of a novel?

4. What does 'genre' mean?

5. It is possible to gain a coursework grade without writing a word. True or False?

5. True. You can be assessed orally.
4. 'Type' – as in romance, Western or detective fiction
3. How it is affected by the time in which it was written
2. Three. One set text and two for coursework
1. Two. One set text and one for coursework

LITERARY TECHNIQUE: NARRATORS, CHARACTERISATION AND DIALOGUE (EN2)

WHAT TO LOOK FOR IN CHARACTERS

When you are studying the characters in your novel, you should look out for the following things.

- The names of characters sometimes tell you more about them. For example, Pip from *Great Expectations* is named after a seed. One of the novel's main themes is his development and growth as he changes from a lower-class boy to a gentleman. The novel charts the education of his heart as well as his mind.

- What characters look like. The physical appearance of characters given in their description often tells us more about them.

- What a character says and does. Much can be inferred from talk and action.

- Flat and round characters. E.M. Forster created these terms to describe types of characters found in novels in his book *Aspects of the Novel* (1927). Flat characters do not develop in novels and are generally not as important as round characters, who develop because they change in the course of a novel. The same terms can be applied to characters in short stories.

- How a character interacts with other characters.

- What other characters say about him or her. This can help readers understand other aspects of a character's personality.

- Any direct comments on the character by a third-person narrator.

- If the character that you are studying is the narrator of your story, how far can you trust what he or she says? Do they have self-knowledge or do they have a lot to learn? Could they be termed an unreliable narrator?

Examiner's Top Tip
Always check to see if a story is written in the first or third person.

FIRST- OR THIRD-PERSON NARRATOR?

- Notice how writers tell their stories. Do they tell the story from the point of view of a character within the story as 'I' or 'me' – that is, as a first-person narrator? Or have they chosen to write about the story from the point of view of someone who looks at what is going on from outside the story and in which the narrator says 'he', 'she' or 'they'? The writer's choice of who tells the story can determine how we see, understand and interpret characters, as well as themes and ideas within a story.

- First-person narrators usually have a limited point of view. They are so close to what is happening that they cannot see everything that is going on or know what other characters are thinking.

- Third-person narrators can see and know much more. They can know everything if the writer wants them to. This last kind of narrator is called an omniscient narrator.

- It is important to understand that whatever the first- or third-person narrator thinks is not necessarily what the writer thinks. Show in your writing that you understand that writers adopt masks by using narrators in their stories.

DIALOGUE

- **Dialogue is speech between two or more characters**. In novels this is more than mere communication; it makes **characters seem more vivid** and **lifelike**.
- Dialogue helps readers **learn** about characters; they reveal their **aims**, **motive**, **personalities** and **outlooks** through what they say and the words and phrases that they use.
- **Dialogue shows what characters think about other characters**. This also helps **us** make up our minds about them and understand how they relate to the main **themes**, **messages** and **ideas** in a story.

An example of third-person narration and characterisation from Doris Lessing's Flight:

He moved warily along the hedge, stalking his granddaughter, who was now looped over the gate, her head loose on her arms, singing. The light happy sound mingled with the crooning of the birds, and his anger mounted.

'Hey!' he shouted; saw her jump, look back, and abandon the gate. Her eyes veiled themselves, and she said in a pert neutral voice: 'Hullo, Grandad.' Politely she moved towards him, after a lingering backward glance at the road.

'Waiting for Steven, hey?' he said, his fingers curling like claws into his palm.

'Any objection?' she asked lightly, refusing to look at him.

He confronted her, his eyes narrowed, shoulders hunched, tight in a hard knot of pain which included the preening birds, the sunlight, the flowers. He said: 'Think you're old enough to go courting, hey?'

An example of first-person narration and dialogue from from Sylvia Plath's Superman and Paula Brown's New Snowsuit.

[The narrator has been wrongfully accused of spoiling Paula Brown's snowsuit.]

A mouthful of chocolate pudding blocked my throat, thick and bitter. I had to wash it down with milk. Finally I said, 'I didn't do it.'

But the words came out like hard, dry little seeds, hollow and insincere. I tried again. 'I didn't do it. Jimmy Lane did it.'

'Of course we'll believe you,' Mother said slowly, 'but the whole neighbourhood is talking about it. Mrs Sterling heard the story from Mrs Fein and sent David over to say we should buy Paula a new snowsuit. I can't understand it.'

'I didn't do it,' I repeated, and the blood beat in my ears like a slack drum. I pushed my chair away from the table, not looking at Uncle Frank or Mother sitting there, solemn and sorrowful in the candlelight.

The staircase to the second floor was dark, but I went down the long hall to my room without turning on the light switch and shut the door. A small unripe moon was shafting squares of greenish light along the floor and the window-panes were fringed with frost.

Examiner's Top Tip
Remember that it is not enough to identify literary terms in texts. You need to comment on their effectiveness.

QUICK TEST

1. In *Flight*, how does the narrator use description of actions to show Grandad's emotions?
2. What do the granddaughter's short answers show about her attitude?
3. In *Superman and Paula Brown's New Snowsuit*, what does the narrator say three times?
4. What does she say about the way she spoke?
5. What does she say about how she felt? What does this show?

5. The blood pounding in her ears shows that she was probably blushing.
4. She says she sounded insincere.
3. 'I didn't do it.'
2. They show that she is being careful not to upset her grandfather.
1. 'Fingers curling like claws' and 'shoulders hunched, tight in a hard knot of pain' show that he is angry.

81

THEMES, MOOD AND ATMOSPHERE AND THE SIMILARITIES AND DIFFERENCES OF NOVELS AND STORIES (EN2)

THEMES

Themes are <u>ideas</u> or <u>messages</u> that writers explore in their stories. The novel is a <u>form</u> of writing that allows writers to use more than one <u>theme</u>.

• In *Roll of Thunder Hear My Cry* (1976), Mildred D. Taylor explores the <u>theme</u> of growing up and the coming of age of its main character, Cassie Logan. She experiences racism in 1930s' Mississippi, despite her family's best efforts to shield her from its worst aspects. Among other <u>themes</u>, the novel also examines <u>the characters' attachment to the land, family roots, independence</u> and the <u>self-respect</u> that comes from owning parcels of land.

MOOD AND ATMOSPHERE

Writers try to create a <u>mood and atmosphere</u> in stories and novels to illuminate the <u>feelings</u> and <u>actions</u> of their characters. <u>Mood</u> and <u>atmosphere</u>, through the skilful use of description, help set the <u>tone</u> for a piece of writing; this creates a frame of mind for the reader and a sense of expectation of what is to follow. <u>Mood and atmosphere</u> can be achieved by using the following <u>literary effects</u>:

• careful choice of words (<u>diction</u>) which helps suggest an <u>atmosphere</u> and <u>tone</u>
• the <u>length</u> and <u>variety</u> of <u>sentences</u>; short ones can suggest tension
• <u>repetition</u> in sentences of words and phrases
• <u>monologues</u> (speaking to oneself); <u>dreams</u> and <u>day-dreams</u> are good ways of revealing the <u>motives</u> and <u>desires</u> of characters
• <u>similes</u>
• <u>metaphors</u>
• <u>personification</u>
• <u>oxymorons</u>
• <u>alliteration</u>
• <u>assonance</u>
• <u>motifs</u> (<u>words, ideas and imagery</u> which recur in texts)
• the use of the <u>senses</u>: <u>sound, touch, sight, smell and touch</u>
• through the <u>tone</u> of the <u>narrator</u> and his or her <u>closeness</u> to, or <u>distance</u> from, the <u>action</u>.

Examiner's Top Tip
Choose a passage that moves you from a text that you are reading and try to work out how the writer created the mood and atmosphere of the passage.

COMPARING NOVELS AND STORIES

- Both have <u>plots</u> and <u>stories</u>.
- Both may include <u>dialogue</u>.
- Both have <u>characters</u>.
- Both set out <u>themes</u> and <u>ideas</u>.

Short stories differ from novels in that they:
- are usually based upon a <u>specific incident</u> or <u>point in time</u>
- usually have just <u>one</u> main plot and they have no space for <u>sub-plots</u> or <u>sub-texts</u>.

- have <u>less description</u> because there is less space: any <u>description</u> used needs to be <u>economical and essential</u> as it has to add meaning to a story.
- <u>use striking details</u>.
- sometimes have more <u>fragmented dialogue</u>
- include <u>fewer characters</u> who do and say more in less space than characters in novels.

LOVE AND LOSS IN *CHEMISTRY* AND *SNOWDROPS*

These two stories have a great deal in common and provide a number of areas that are worth exploring in depth.

MAIN IDEAS

Both stories centre on a young boy who is a witness to other people's sorrows. The narrator in *Chemistry* and the boy in *Snowdrops* (neither character is given a name) observe the life that goes on around them and try to make sense of it. Central to both stories is a death. In *Chemistry* the narrator is deeply affected by the death of his grandfather, whilst the boy in *Snowdrops* is a silent witness to his teacher's reaction to the death of her boyfriend.

THEME

The main theme is loss. In *Chemistry* all of the central characters suffer a loss. The Grandfather has lost his wife, the mother has lost her husband and the narrator eventually loses his Grandfather. The first two deaths bring the three central characters together and there is an initial period of harmony in the story. The arrival of Ralph, the mother's new lover, disturbs this harmony and eventually leads to the death of the Grandfather. In *Snowdrops* the death of Miss Webster's boyfriend causes a small disruption to the boy's routine as a promised treat is delayed, presumably by her attendance at the church service held for him. At that time in Wales only men attended the funeral and so Miss Webster is able to return to school in time for the treat of showing her class some early snowdrops. The boy sees his teacher's distress as her boyfriend's funeral passes near the school.

SYMBOLS

Both stories use powerful symbols. The harmonious period in *Chemistry* is represented by the Grandfather, mother and boy sailing a boat on a local pond. Significantly the boat sinks at about the same time as Ralph appears. The Grandfather says of the loss, 'You must accept it – it's the only way'. Later the boy's father appears to him in a dream and blames the mother for his own death by water. At the end of the story the boy returns to the pond and sees a vision of his Grandfather. He realises that things are only changed and not destroyed and that his Grandfather and his boat continue to exist beyond the surface of the pond – here symbolising death. In *Snowdrops* the boy is very excited at the prospect of going to see the flowers but is at first disappointed by the reality. On reflection he comes to understand the bravery and strength of the snowdrops as they bring a touch of beauty and a promise of spring to an otherwise harsh winter world. Like the music that accompanies the passing funeral, this is a sad and beautiful truth.

NARRATIVE TECHNIQUE

Chemistry is told in the first person and covers incidents that take place over a period of three or four years. The narrator is ten years old at the end of the story and has only a limited understanding of adult feelings and motivation. He records incidents that are significant to him but the reader often has a better understanding of what is going on than the child. *Snowdrops* has a third-person narrator and records the events of a single day. The narrator adopts the boy's point of view and records events as he sees them. The boy overhears, for instance, an adult conversation that allows the reader to understand the teacher's situation but it is clear that the boy does not make any connection between what he has heard and the late arrival of his teacher. Both stories thus work on two levels. They record the children's views of the world but provide the reader with enough information to see beyond the innocent eyes of their central characters.

SHORT STORIES

The NEAB Anthology contains the following stories.

Flight by Doris Lessing

An old man who keeps pigeons worries that his granddaughter is going to go away and leave him. At the start of the story he locks his favourite pigeon up but he releases it when Steven gives him a new bird. The story ends on an ambiguous note with Alice in tears after observing the release.

Superman and Paula Brown's New Snowsuit by Sylvia Plath

The story is set during the Second World War. A young girl, wrongfully accused of spoiling Paula Brown's snowsuit, is deeply upset when her mother and uncle do not immediately believe that she is innocent. The moment marks the end of one phase of her childhood.

Your Shoes by Michèle Roberts

A mother sits in her fifteen year-old daughter's room. The daughter has run away and the mother thinks about their relationship. She holds a pair of the daughter's shoes as a reminder of the missing girl.

Growing Up Joyce Carey

A father returns home to find his daughter's twelve- and thirteen year-old daughters in the garden. They ignore him and tease the family dog. When the father intervenes, he is bitten and the two girls take charge. Later, the girls help at a committee meeting at the house. The father thinks about the changing roles and moods of his children.

The End of Something by Ernest Hemmingway

A young man and young woman go fishing together. As they camp in the evening the young man tells the woman that he has 'taught her everything' and that the fun has gone out of their relationship. The woman leaves. The young man stays by the fire, and when a friend arrives and asks how his break-up went, the young man does not wish to talk about it.

Chemistry by Graham Swift

A boy, his widowed mother and his grandfather live together in harmony in the grandfather's house. They sail a model boat on the local pond. The harmony is disturbed by the arrival of Ralph. The grandfather becomes increasingly isolated and retires to his shed where he makes models and studies chemistry. Eventually, the grandfather commits suicide leaving the mother, son and Ralph to begin a new life. The son reflects on loss and its causes.

Snowdrops by Leslie Noris

A six year-old boy at a Welsh school eagerly anticipates being taken to see some snowdrops. On the morning of this 'treat' he hears that his teacher's boyfriend has been killed in a motorcycle accident. The teacher arrives late for school and the treat is delayed until the afternoon. At first the boy is disappointed when he sees the snowdrops but begins to understand the strength they need to appear so early in the year. As he looks up to tell his teacher, he notices that she is crying. Her boyfriend's funeral is passing the school.

Making connections

As you can see from the above summaries, all of the short stories concern children or young people.

Flight, *The End of Something*, *Growing Up* and *Your Shoes* are about adolescents and teenagers. The dominant theme here, with the exception of *The End of Something*, is achieving <u>independence</u> <u>from</u> <u>adults</u>.

Superman and Paula Brown's New Snowsuit, *Snowdrops* and *Chemistry* all look at the world from <u>a child's</u> <u>point</u> <u>of</u> <u>view</u>.

All of the stories involve <u>change</u> <u>and</u> <u>transition</u>.

SHORT STORIES IN THE EXAM

If you are studying a novel, you only have that text to write about. If you have followed the short story option, you will have to compare and contrast one story with another. Many people find it is easier to talk about one thing if they have something else to compare it with.

You will be asked to compare short stories in terms of:

- content
- **characters**
- theme
- **setting**
- style

The two most popular areas for comparison are character and theme, followed by plot. There is also a chance of getting a question on style in this part of the exam. A typical question might look like this:

In both *Superman and Paula Brown's New Snowsuit* and *Growing Up* the main characters learn things about people around them. Compare the things they learn, and the ways the writers show the characters' experiences of learning. Write about:
- the things they learn
- how the writers show the characters' experiences of learning by the ways they write about them
- similarities and differences between their experiences of learning, and how the writers show them.

Sometimes, as here, you will be given the titles of both short stories; sometimes you will be given one title and asked to choose a second. Occasionally you will be able to choose both stories.

AN ESSAY PLAN

QUESTION

In both *Snowdrops* and *Chemistry* the main characters see things that they don't fully understand. Compare the experiences of the two characters and the ways the writers make use of their innocent vision.

Examiner's Top Tip
You will probably have your favourites amongst the stories you have studied but in most years you will have no choice about at least one of them. This means you need to revise all the stories equally.

PROVIDE BACKGROUND
Compare and contrast the backgrounds of the two characters showing your knowledge of social and historical context.

WHAT DO THE TWO CHARACTERS UNDERSTAND BY THE END OF THE STORIES?
Compare and contrast the attitudes of the two boys at the end.

DISCUSS THE USE OF SYMBOLS
Compare and contrast the use made of the launch and lake with the use of the snowdrops.

EXPLAIN WHAT THE BOYS OBSERVE AND WHAT THEY FAIL TO UNDERSTAND
Compare and contrast the ways in which the authors allow the reader to understand what the boys don't.

CONCLUSION
Give your views on the stories and what you learned.

EXAM QUESTIONS - Use the questions to test your progress. Check your answers on page 95.

How to Study Novels and Short Stories

1. What type assessment is used for novels in the English syllabus?
....

2. What is the cut-off date for older novels?
....

3. If you are studying an older novel, what do you have to check about the author?
....

4. What is the historical context of a text?
....

5. Are you assessed on reading or writing?
....

6. What does 'plot' mean?
....

7. What does it mean to 'contrast'?
....

8. Explain the term 'genre'.
....

9. What is meant by a 'writer's craft'?
....

10. Explain what irony means.
....

11. What are 'transitions'?
....

12. Give two types of themes that you may write about in your assignments.
....

Literary Technique: Narrators, Characterisation and Dialogue

13. What are the main styles of narration?
....

14. From which viewpoint does a first-person narrator tell a story?
....

15. Does the author believe what a narrator believes?
....

16. What type of narrator can see most in a story?
....

17. Give three ways of understanding a character.
....

18. What is an 'omniscient narrator'?
....

19. What is meant by the terms 'flat' and 'round' characters?
....

20. Define what dialogue means.

....

21. Why do writers use dialogue?

....

22. Briefly explain the rules for how dialogue should be set out on the page.

....

23. What is a monologue?

....

24. How can dialogue help you learn more about characters?

....

Themes, Atmosphere and the Differences between Novels and Stories

25. Identify three similarities in novels and short stories.

....

26. Point out three differences between short stories and novels.

....

27. Why do short stories concentrate on mainly one plot?

....

28. Point out three ways in which writers create mood and atmosphere in their stories.

....

29. What is 'diction'?

....

30. Mood and atmosphere sets up a frame of mind and an expectation of what is to follow in a text. True or false?

....

31. Mood and atmosphere can be achieved through the skilful use of description or imagery. True or false?

....

32. Imagery is used only for poetry and not in novels or short stories. True or false?

....

33. Explain the difference between alliteration and assonance.

....

34. What is a theme?

....

35. Give one example of a theme that can be linked with the historical context of a novel or a story.

....

36. Briefly sum up the difference between a short story and a novel.

....

How did you do?

1–9	correct	start again
10–19	correct	getting there
20–29	correct	good work
30–36	correct	excellent

ARE YOU ON STUDY LEAVE?

- The <u>secret</u> <u>of</u> <u>success</u> is to do a <u>little</u> <u>and</u> <u>often</u> every day. Assign yourself <u>set</u> <u>times</u> to do your revision. Why not stick to the times you would have used to attend your English lessons in school?
- <u>Get</u> <u>together</u> <u>with</u> <u>a</u> <u>friend</u> and share the burden by covering different parts of your revision and then <u>discussing</u> <u>your</u> <u>findings</u>. You will also help <u>motivate</u> each other.
- For essay plans <u>brainstorm</u> your ideas and then <u>write</u> <u>numbers</u> around your <u>brainstormed</u> <u>plan</u> so that you can <u>list</u> <u>your</u> <u>ideas</u> <u>in</u> <u>the</u> <u>best</u> <u>order</u>. This will give your essay <u>a</u> <u>logical</u>, <u>fluent</u> <u>structure</u>. Ask a friend to mark your work and correct any <u>punctuation</u> <u>mistakes</u>. Improve your <u>proof-reading</u> <u>skills</u> by marking the work of friends.

PLANNING AND READING IN EXAMS

- <u>Do</u> <u>not</u> <u>panic</u>! Channel all your <u>nervous</u> <u>energy</u> and <u>adrenaline</u> into your exam. If you are answering questions on poetry, <u>find</u> <u>the</u> <u>questions</u> <u>that</u> <u>apply</u> <u>to</u> <u>you</u> and do the ones that you think that you can answer best.
- <u>Question</u> <u>the</u> <u>question</u>. <u>Read</u> <u>the</u> <u>questions</u> <u>very</u> carefully and <u>underline</u> <u>key</u> <u>words</u> and <u>phrases</u>. Think about these as you read your passages.
- <u>Read</u> <u>through</u> written passages <u>twice</u>: <u>firstly</u> to get <u>the</u> <u>gist</u> of the <u>meaning</u> and <u>then</u> <u>for</u> <u>deeper</u> <u>understanding</u>. Carefully read the passages and <u>note</u> <u>the</u> <u>development</u> <u>of</u> <u>arguments</u> <u>and</u> <u>ideas</u> as well as how they are expressed by <u>underlining</u> <u>words</u> or by <u>making</u> <u>short</u>, <u>phrase-like</u> <u>notes</u>.
- <u>Brainstorm</u> <u>a</u> <u>brief</u> <u>five-point</u> (or so) <u>plan</u> and then <u>re-number</u> <u>your</u> <u>points</u> in the order that you will need to write them (this will help your <u>structure</u>).

WHEN YOU WRITE EXAM ANSWERS

- <u>Do</u> <u>not</u> <u>waste</u> <u>time</u> <u>with</u> <u>long</u> <u>introductions</u> – get straight into your answer with only <u>a</u> <u>brief</u> <u>introduction</u>, setting out your answer and remembering to use <u>standard</u> <u>English</u>. That is, make sure that your <u>writing</u> <u>is</u> <u>formal</u> and <u>avoid</u> <u>abbreviations</u>, unless you are asked to use <u>dialect</u>.

- Show your understanding of texts by <u>reading</u> <u>between</u> <u>the</u> <u>lines</u> and by <u>putting</u> <u>information</u> <u>in</u> <u>your</u> <u>own</u> <u>words</u>. Remember to use <u>brief</u> <u>quotations</u> <u>as</u> <u>evidence</u> for your points and <u>integrate</u> <u>them</u> <u>within</u> <u>your</u> <u>writing</u>. Constantly refer back to the question, when writing, and ask yourself, 'Am I being <u>relevant</u> here?' and, 'Am I using <u>key</u> <u>words</u> <u>from</u> <u>the</u> <u>question</u> in my answer.'

- <u>Add</u> <u>points</u> <u>to</u> <u>your</u> <u>plan</u> <u>while</u> <u>writing</u> in case you forget them. Your brain is remarkable because you can think of two things at once. Do not lose track of good ideas as you write your answers. Simply <u>break</u> <u>off</u> <u>from</u> <u>your</u> <u>answer</u> and <u>add</u> the necessary points to your plan.

- Be <u>ruthless</u> and divide your time <u>sensibly</u> according to the marks at stake for each <u>question</u>. Do not get bogged down looking for an extra one or two marks when there is a <u>fresh</u> <u>question</u> with <u>several</u> <u>marks</u> at stake. You should be trying to <u>average</u> a high number of marks for each question. Do not unbalance your effort by trying to get the maximum mark for any single question. You must <u>spread</u> <u>your</u> <u>effort</u> and <u>aim</u> <u>for</u> <u>an</u> <u>overall</u> <u>mark</u> <u>in</u> <u>your</u> <u>answers</u>. That is a <u>successful</u> <u>technique</u>.

- <u>Your</u> <u>aim</u> <u>is</u> <u>to</u> <u>build</u> <u>up</u> <u>marks</u> <u>in</u> <u>each</u> <u>answer</u> and to share your effort efficiently. A paragraph or so with bullet points is fine for six marks but you will need <u>several</u> paragraphs for a 26-mark question. Again, be careful not to spend <u>too</u> <u>long</u> on questions with few marks at stake.

- <u>Managing</u> <u>your</u> <u>time</u> <u>is</u> <u>crucial</u> <u>in</u> <u>exams</u>. Allow yourself five to 10 minutes to check your work through for errors of <u>sense</u>, <u>spelling</u> and <u>punctuation</u>. Ask yourself, 'What errors do I usually make?'

FIVE POINTS TO REMEMBER ON THE WORDING OF WRITING EXAM QUESTIONS

In exam questions to:
1. explain means to show knowledge and understanding by giving a detailed account of something
2. describe means to set forth the characteristics or details of something
3. argue is to maintain a stand-point through logic as you would in an essay
4. inform means to show an understanding of something by giving a clear account of it to someone else
5. advise is similar to inform: it means to teach someone or a particular audience something as clearly as you can.

EXAM TECHNIQUE AND GENERAL ADVICE

FIVE POINTS TO REMEMBER ABOUT WORDS AND PHRASES IN READING EXAM QUESTIONS

1. Use of language means word choices, emotive words and phrases to affect the audience, description, persuasive phrases, imagery, alliteration, etc. Avoid saying that the language used 'is very good' which suggests you do not know what to say.
2. Style of presentation means how the text is set out. Think about the text's form. For instance, is it a letter or a newspaper article? Think about the use of underlining, bullet points, statistics, graphs and pictures. How do each of these devices express meaning and aid understanding?
3. The attitude to the reader is the 'tone of voice' adopted by the writer. Is it, for example, polite, ironic, formal, informal, serious, comic, academic, sarcastic, etc. The tone a writer chooses is always important for the purpose of any piece of writing.
4. Convey means to get across. For example, 'How does the writer convey a sense of . . .'
5. Compare and contrast means: 'What is similar?' and 'What is different?'

PRACTICE QUESTIONS

Questions for 30-minute exam practice for the poetry sections of the exam.

Poets in the English National Heritage

1. Write about two poems that interested you. Explain why.

2. Examine the presentation of characters in at least two poems.

Poetry From Different Cultures

1. Compare two poems that are linked by a similar theme.

2. Compare and contrast two poems from this section.

Examiner's Top Tip
Use your time effectively. In the NEAB Paper 1 you have two hours to get 108 marks. Excluding planning time, that works out at almost a mark a minute.

THE READING SECTIONS

WHAT YOU SHOULD HAVE REVISED

- Find the **relevant** stories or poems that you have been studying in class. **Do not write about poems and poets that you have not studied**. This seems an obvious point yet a number of pupils each year write about poems, etc. that they have never studied. The poetry section in the English Exam is worth **15%** of your final mark.

- Remember that time will be **limited**. For example, in the AQA exam **you only have 45 minutes** to answer the questions for your prepared poetry from different cultures. Other exam boards will also set short time limits on their **pre-released reading materials**, so it is important to be **relevant** in your answers and to **use appropriate evidence for your points**.

- You should have revised **key themes that link your poems or stories together**. The best way to see which texts go together is to **produce a chart with the poems down one side and the themes at the top**. Briefly point out any connections between the themes in your squares; you will then see which texts to pair up and write about in exams.

- This is even more important in the AQA Literature exam when you have four poems to consider.

WHEN YOU BEGIN WRITING

- Write about <u>links</u> between the poems or stories and <u>show your awareness of the main similarities and differences</u>.

- If you are doing the <u>Foundation</u> paper use the <u>bullet points</u>, which your exam board has provided for you under your question. You may not be able to answer all the bullet points in the time allowed. You should then aim to do <u>three out of four</u> bullet points and <u>do them as well as you can</u>. Examiners are looking for <u>understanding</u>, <u>knowledge</u> and <u>relevance</u>, rather than long answers in which pupils try to say everything that they know.

- The advice is the same for anyone doing the <u>Higher</u> paper, only <u>you have to brainstorm your own four- or five-point plan from the question</u>. You should <u>number the points in your plan</u> afterwards to help you produce a <u>structured</u> and <u>fluent</u> answer. Remember that you cannot, and should not, say everything that you know about your chosen poems. You will probably only use around 25% of your knowledge so it is vital to be <u>relevant</u> and <u>focus</u> your answer on <u>key words and phrases from your question</u>.

- <u>Facts</u> are things that <u>can be proved</u>, for example, 'Chelsea FC won the FA Cup in 2000'.

- <u>Opinions cannot be proved</u> because they are subjective. For example, 'Chelsea FC will win the Premier League for the next three seasons!'

- <u>Be wary of facts dressed up as opinions</u>. For example, 'Chelsea have a policy of buying only foreign players because they have so many of them in their team.'

HOW TO ANSWER QUESTIONS ON UNSEEN, NON-FICTION AND MEDIA TEXTS DURING YOUR EXAMS (EN2)

- **Reading, including the poetry section, is worth 30% of your final mark**. Unseen non-fiction includes: passages, extracts or articles. Once you establish the **form and purpose of the writing**, you will then be able to produce a more **detailed answer in which you later show how a writer either informs or persuades their audience**.
- **There are three main questions to ask of any text**:
1. What kind of writing is this? Is the writing meant to **entertain**, **inform**, **persuade**, etc.
2. What is the **form** of the writing? Is it **an article**, **leaflet**, **letter**, **biography**, etc? Does the writer use the **first** or **third** person? The **second-person** form of **'you'** is often used in junk mail. Remember that **layout** and **images** are an important way of **getting messages across**. Be prepared to comment on their effectiveness, especially when you are asked to **compare** one text with another.
3. What does the text **mean** to you? What are your **motives** for reading this text? Do you **share** its values? How will you **interpret** it? What does it make you **think**?

   In other words:
   1. What is the writer trying to say?
   2. What means does he or she employ towards effective communication?
   3. How successful is the writer in achieving his or her aims?

TIPS ON PERSUASIVE TECHNIQUES

Look again at the Media pages of this book on 'How To Analyse A Media Text' for fuller advice on persuasive techniques. You could use any variation of them in your answers on passages or in your own piece of writing.

Rhetorical questions: these are designed to involve an audience and make them think about an issue.

Personal testimony: brief quotations from experts or witnesses can be used to verify arguments and make them appear more valid.

Emotive language: words and phrases that can make you feel strongly about someone or something.

Repetition: this is a form of rhetoric in which you repeat key phrases in your arguments. For example:

Formatting: underlining, bullet points, statistics, the use of colour, capital letters, bold print, graphics and well-chosen pictures with captions can also play an important part in persuading an audience and make information easier to grasp.

PERSUASIVE TECHNIQUES ARE PARTICULARLY USEFUL FOR EXAMS

Firstly, secondly, and thirdly . . . Dr Martin Luther King famously repeated the phrase 'I have a dream' to great effect in his speech for equality outside the White House in 1968.

Humour: when this is used in a controlled way to undermine an opposing point of view it can be very effective.

Fonts and type sizes: these are often carefully selected to give points more impact or carry other associations that advertisers would like you to think.

QUICK TEST

1. How much time do you have for your answer in the poetry section?
2. What is the second person and where would you find it?
3. What is a fact?
4. Is this a fact or an opinion: 'Animal experimentation is wrong.'
5. What is emotive language?

5. Words and phrases which are meant to make you feel strongly about something
4. An opinion
3. Something that you can prove
2. You. Mostly in junk mail, sales literature etc.
1. 45 minutes

HOW TO PRODUCE A PIECE OF WRITING WORTHY OF A HIGH GRADE

You will need to do the following to produce a good answer.

• **Plan** your writing.

• Focus on your **purpose** (what you want your **audience** to know).

• **Consider** **your** **audience** and use an appropriate language and tone.

• **Use** **varied** **sentence** **structure** and punctuation, as well as showing clarity of thought.

• Develop points into logical, well-constructed **paragraphs** with **topic** **sentences**.

• Use a variety of **linking** **words** (conjunctions) to help you signpost your points.

• Show **accuracy** in your **spelling** and **punctuation**.

• **Proof-read** your work and **correct** **it** where necessary. Teachers and examiners love to see evidence of **proof-reading** because it shows that pupils have attained a level of maturity as **independent** **learners**.

WRITING TO ARGUE, PERSUADE OR ADVISE

This **is** **worth** **15%** **of** **your** **final** **mark.**

• *Audience and purpose*
The first thing to do is consider your purpose and then focus on how you can best persuade your particular audience.

• *Form*
Select an appropriate form: a letter, newspaper article, pamphlet, leaflet, essay, etc.

• *Planning*
Always plan your writing. A brief brainstormed plan (perhaps in the form of a spidergram) can later be numbered to help you order and shape your writing.

• *Use appropriate language and register*
All formal writing needs to be written in standard English.

• *Be convincing*
If you are writing a letter of complaint, try to avoid sounding pompous, strident or foolishly outraged. You must build instead a reasonable case that is based on as much evidence as you can muster.

WRITING TO ADVISE, INFORM, EXPLAIN OR DESCRIBE

This **is** **worth** **15%** **of** **your** **final** **mark.**

• This could be anything from composing a letter informing parents of a school trip to composing a leaflet setting out the dangers of tooth decay for primary school-aged pupils.

• The choice of topic that you will be asked to write about will be determined by the material that you read earlier in the exam. So if you had read articles or information pamphlets on tooth decay, you will have a number of facts, statistics, opinions, arguments and evidence to draw upon. But beware of simply repeating sentences and paragraphs that you have previously read. That is plagiarism. Process the information by putting it in your own words and by giving credit to the other writers by citing (giving) their names and the titles of the articles in your work.

• Foundation papers will help you by providing a brief plan for your writing with helpful advice. If you are taking the higher paper you will then have to brainstorm your own. Remember that writing which is planned is better than that which is unplanned. There is simply more fluency, structure and detail in planned writing. You will also avoid head-scratching in the middle of your exam if you have thought about your writing in the first five to 10 minutes of your answer.

• Exam boards these days are not overly concerned with the form in which pupils' writing is set out: it is what is said and how it is expressed that is more important. In other words, you do not have to worry about making, for instance, a newspaper article look like one. You should try, however, to adopt the written style of a journalist.

PRACTICE QUESTIONS FOR BOTH TYPES OF WRITING IN THE EXAM

You usually get <u>an hour</u> for these sections of the papers. Try some of the following ideas for exam practice at home.

Examiner's Top Tip
Ask your teacher for past exam papers so that you can get a feel for how they are laid out and for the type of questions you may be asked.

PAPER 1. WRITING TO ARGUE, PERSUADE OR ADVISE

- Argue for or against blood sports or animal experimentation for an audience of your own age.
- Write a pamphlet on the dangers of under-age drinking or smoking for a younger audience.
- Prepare a detailed list of instructions for organising a prize-giving evening for teachers.
- Write an article for young people in which you argue for or against the effects of watching television.

PAPER 2. WRITING TO INFORM, EXPLAIN OR DESCRIBE

- Write an explanation of your favourite hobby for a beginner.
- Describe your ideal teacher.
- Look at sections of magazines that show a day in the life of someone. Write about a typical day in your life and entitle it 'A Life In The Day of . . . '.
- Write about an event that changed your outlook on life.

THE WRITING SECTIONS

The two writing sections of the exams are worth 30% of your final mark – 15% in Paper 1 and 15% in Paper 2.

Five Points to Remember

1. You have one hour for each section of writing.
2. Plan your writing. Spend between five to 10 minutes making your plan.
3. Number the points in your plan so that your writing has fluency and structure.
4. Signpost your arguments and points with a variety of connectives.
5. Match your style of writing to your chosen form.

QUICK TEST

1. Why is it important to plan your writing?
2. Should you use abbreviations in your writing?
3. What must you always do once you complete a piece of writing?
4. What are the two main factors to consider when producing a piece of writing for the exam?
5. How much of your final grade depends on the writing sections of the exam?

Examiner's Top Tip
Improve your persuasive skills by reading sophisticated junk-mail letters and pamphlets. Try to spot seven techniques each time.

5. 30%
4. You must consider the purpose and target audience for your writing.
3. Proof-read your work for punctuation, spelling, clarity and sense.
2. No. Stick with standard English. Only use dialect if it is asked for.
1. It will have more detail and be more structured.

Punctuation and Speaking and Listening

Punctuation and Sentences

1. You need to punctuate your work so that your readers will fully understand your meaning.
2. Check your answer against page 7. (Award yourself a mark if you got all five.)
3. Jemma, *Great Expectations*, English, the first She, Charles Dickens and Easter.
4. Full stop, semi-colon, colon, exclamation mark and question mark.
5. They join closely related sentences; they separate sets of items in lists when there are commas within the sets or lists.
6. A question to which you do not expect a direct answer. You expect instead that your listener will agree with you.
7. Colons can introduce a list; they can introduce a sentence which expands upon the meaning of the first sentence; they can also introduce long quotations that are separated from the writer's prose.
8. Inverted commas are needed for words spoken; the speech needs to be separated from the rest of the writing by a punctuation mark; it is introduced with a capital letter; you need a new line for each speaker; and each new line should be indented three spaces from the margin.
9. Apostrophes can indicate possession or an abbreviated word or phrase.
10. Before the 's' as with the firemen's equipment.
11. Statements, exclamations, instructions or commands and questions.
12. The main clause is 'I will go to the cinema'. The dependent clause is 'as soon as I have done the washing up'.

Spelling and Expression

13. Spelling phonetically sounding out each syllable:
Look–Cover–Say
Write–Check
Use a dictionary; produce a mnemonic.
14. It is 'i' before 'e' except after 'c'.
15. There is a consonant before the 'y' as with 'city'; so it's 'cities'.
16. There is a vowel before the 'y' as with 'monkey'; so it's 'monkeys'.
17. They are all to do with place.
18. Beginning, appearance, interested, grammar, tongue, definitely, necessity, rhythm, sentence.
19. Synonyms are words that mean the same.
20. Homophones are words that are different yet sound the same. For instance, 'whether' and 'weather'.
21. Connective words link phrases, sentences and paragraphs together.
22. To help signpost ideas and arguments so that readers can follow what you mean.

23. Paragraphs break up forbidding chunks of text and make meaning clear. Writers need them to organise their main points and ideas.
24. The topic sentence is the main sentence in a paragraph. The remaining sentences expand on its meaning.
25. 'Control' is the ability to write sentences and paragraphs of appropriate length with control over expression. Word choices and punctuation will also be appropriate and accurate.
26. Because.

Speaking and Listening

27. Three.
28. Single, paired and group orals.
29. Local speech particular to an area. It is informal speech.
30. Cockney, Geordie, Scouse, Brummie. There are many others!
31. Formal English used by teachers, doctors, lawyers, in business, etc.
32. Use local dialect with your friends and family. This is because it is friendly and informal; use standard English in formal situations to people with whom you are doing business and do not know.
33. You should note details such as the type of oral and the topic; you will need the date, some notes on your preparation; you should record how the oral went by making a self-assessment so you can set targets for your next oral.
34. Non-verbal language such as eye contact, hand gestures, etc.
35. Register is the tone you adopt when addressing various audiences; for example you should speak to a judge than you would to a friend.
36. We are being ironic if the tone of our voices implies the opposite meaning of words we use.
37. Good listeners have better, more complex conversations. They have good turn-taking skills too.
38. To 'work out', to 'unpick', to 'unravel'.
39. Debates, topical issues in the news; or an issue that came out of a class text.
40. You are assessed on your ability to talk, not to read. Long, written passages prevent fluency in speech because of the temptation to look at them for reassurance.
41. The 'structure' of your talk is the clarity and order of its presentation.
42. Self-assessment is crucial for setting new targets for improvement and achieving them.

Writing and the Media

1. Writing.
2. Around 1000 words.
3. Story line.

4. Kind of writing. For example, detective or horror stories.
5. The use 'as' or 'like' in the comparison.
6. An interesting beginning which draws the reader in.
7. The setting is where the story is supposed to be in time and place.
8. Check your answer with 'What You Can Write About' on page 31.
9. Writing that you have created yourself.
10. First and third person.
11. Third person.
12. The plan or outline of the story.
13. Notes, brainstorm or spidergram.
14. Fluency of expression and punctuation.
15. Linear is a 'straight line'. There is no going backwards or forwards as the story unfolds. For example, *Romeo and Juliet* is a linear play because the action takes place over four days.

Personal Writing: Non-fiction

16. Not made up.
17. Check your answer with 'What You Can Write About' on page 34. Any similar matches will be fine.
18. It means 'to ramble'. You could write about anything.
19. You can get information from knowledgeable people, libraries, the Internet, encyclopedias, companies, embassies, etc.
20. No.
21. The intended audience. Some authors target their novels at early readers; others go for the 10- to 14-year-old market.
22. Newspaper and magazine articles, leaflets, advertising posters, letters, petitions, proclamations, essays, reviews, etc. Anything like these would be fine.
23. Any piece of writing.
24. Instructions for: making a meal; finding directions to somewhere; putting a computer together; a booklet on how to keep fit, etc. Anything like this.
25. Yes.
26. To 'compare' is to examine what is similar; to 'contrast' is to say what is different.
27. The 'historical context' includes the events and ideas present at the time when the text was written or set.
28. You need a plan, an introduction, main body and a conclusion. It helps if you have a consistent argument too.
29. At the end of your essay.
30. This is essay technique: you make a 'point', give some appropriate 'evidence' for your point and 'comment', if you can do so.

The Media

31. A number of industries which transmit or 'mediate' information

or entertainment in one form or another. These include the cinema, television, radio, record companies, advertising, the Internet, etc.
32. All possibilities are too numerous to mention. They range from writing a radio script, analysing an advert, reviewing a film, to producing promotional resources for a pop band. Use common sense for your mark.
33. a) illustrations of any kind.
b) a large-size newspaper such as *The Guardian*.
c) the design and look of the page
d) a photo showing the face and sometimes the shoulders
e) large adverts with illustrations
34. a) the name of the journalist
b) only one paper carries the story
c) an emotional story perhaps on success or tragedy
d) the main part of the story
e) the main story on the front page
35. Check your answer against 'A Framework for Looking at Texts' on page 39.
36. Check your answer with the 'Use of Language' on page 40. If your answer is credible give yourself a mark.
37. Usually a catchy line which promotes a product. For instance, BT's is: 'It's good to talk'.
38. They create logos to promote their company image. Logos enable them to be easily recognised by consumers.
39. Check your answers throughout against 'Presentation and Layout' on page 41.
40. 'You', 'Dear Homeowner' and 'Dear Friend'.

Shakespeare

The Shakespeare Assignment

1. Check 'What you may study' on page 48 for possible suggestions. You may study other Shakespeare plays.
2. Read passages for general understanding or the gist first; then read for deeper meaning.
3. Check your answer with 'What you have to do' on page 49. There are other possibilities too.
4. Words and phrases cited from the play (text) as evidence in your writing.
5. Yes.
6. People produce new readings and interpretations of texts according to ideas and values, considered to be important in their time.
7. Imagery and the use of alliteration, assonance, onomatopoeia, etc.
8. History, Tragedy and Comedy. There is a sub-genre: Tragi-comedy.
9. What was then thought about the principles underlying human conduct and nature; how people

thought the world worked, beliefs, etc.

10. Poetic verse, blank verse and prose.
11. For the end of scenes and scenes of dramatic intensity.
12. To show dignified speech; speech that helps convey feeling and mood.

Structure and Themes

13. A sense of normality and order. 'All is well with the world'.
14. Problems are introduced and order begins to break down.
15. The point of highest dramatic intensity before the protagonist's fall.
16. Battles, unmasking, deaths, marriages etc.
17. Order is restored and the right people are back in control.
18. A central idea or ideas.
19. Check your answers with those in 'Some Themes, Ideas, or Messages which recur throughout the plays' on page 50. There are other themes.
20. Love, appearance and reality, good and evil, identity and disguise, etc.
21. A comic scene is followed by a serious scene.
22. This makes a scene appear even more intense or light-hearted because of the contrasting emotions of the previous scene.
23. Self-knowledge is the ability to see learn from your faults when others point them out to you. Characters who do so 'develop'.
24. Order – problems – chaos – climax – resolution with new order.

Imagery and Essay Plans

25. Any kind of imagery or decorative language with alliteration, etc.
26. A comparison using 'as' or 'like'. For instance, 'Clare is like a flower'.
27. It is a comparison which implies or states that something is something else: 'Clare is a flower'.
28. A metaphor that runs or is 'extended' over several lines or a scene.
29. It means 'person-making'. It is powerful metaphor in which things or ideas are given human traits for an enhanced literary effect.
30. Two opposite nouns yoked together for effect: 'A Hard Day's Night'.
31. A character, theme or image that recurs.
32. Imagery helps say more about points made in dialogue and action. It reinforces and enhances the audience's ideas of the characters. It can magnify or draw attention to themes/issues in the text.
33. Characters speak with irony when they say something that is truer than they realise.
34. It is dramatically ironic when the audience knows something important that characters do not. Sometimes

this is complicated by one character knowing what another does with the audience sharing their knowledge.
35. Passages and scenes of dramatic intensity. An example is where Romeo first speaks with Juliet.
36. It includes figurative language, including word-pictures like similes and metaphors.

Poetry

How to Read and Study Poetry

1. Four.
2. Reading.
3. Free-verse, quatrains, couplets, sonnets etc.
4. At least three.
5. The attitude of the narrator to his or her topic and to the reader.
6. First and third person.
7. True.
8. A key message or idea.
9. False. It is a stanza.
10. Carol Ann Duffy
11. False. It is a simile.
12. Seamus Heaney.

How to Write About Poems

13. Two or more. Do not write about too many as your comments could be too thinly stretched.
14. A run-on line. Poets use them for effect.
15. To 'compare' is to note what is 'similar'; to 'contrast' is to explain what is different.
16. A figure of speech and a paradox in which two contradictory terms are brought together for an effect: 'awfully nice' and 'alone together'.
17. Usually mixed feelings or a paradox.
18. True. They are composed of two couplets.
19. Stanzas of irregular length and number.
20. It is an ideal form for conversation and argument.
21. Repetition of vowel sounds for an effect.
22. At the end of your essay. Do give your views because examiners are interested in what you think.

Texts from Different Cultures

23. These are texts written by speakers of English. The poets and writers use either local dialect or standard English in their texts and they mostly come from parts of the world where Britain once had a colonial influence.
24. Free-verse.
25. Glaswegian and West Indian. Or English dialects from any other part of the world.
26. Check what you have studied with the syllabus of your exam board. The AQA Anthology concentrates only on poetry with 'Poems from Different Cultures'. Several of the other exam boards include short stories as well as poems.
27. Check your answers against the information on page 68.
28. Comment on it.

29. True.
30. True.
31. Free verse is the most natural form for conversation and argument.
32. John Agard thinks that the unthinking use of the terms and phrases such as `half-caste' can lead to a racist viewpoint of seeing people of mixed race as only half human and unworthy of being treated as equals.
33. Half an hour.
34. Most of them. If you are with another exam board, do any of the themes mentioned in `Finding Links between the Poems' on page 68 apply to your texts? Try to make a couple of connections and give yourself a mark.
35. Two.
36. One.

Novels and Short Stories
How to Study Novels and Short Stories

1. Coursework.
2. 1914.
3. If he or she is on the National Curriculum list.
4. The time and events which took place when it was written.
5. Reading. However, you will need good writing skills to show your understanding.
6. The outline or structure of a piece of writing.
7. To explain what is different.
8. This refers to the kind or type of writing. For example, romance, adventure, detective, horror, etc.
9. How the writer creates effects through emotive or figurative writing.
10. Saying one thing while meaning another. Also speaking the truth without knowing it.
11. Connectives which allow you to move from one argument or point to another in a fluent manner. They are often key words or phrases that are needed at the beginning of paragraphs such as 'similarly' or 'on the other hand'.
12. Anything from 'Possible Assignments' on page 75 would do for this answer. Anything sensible will be good enough for a mark.

Literary Technique: Narrators, Characterisation and Dialogue

13. First and third person.
14. He or she uses 'I' because they are in the story.
15. Not necessarily. Do not confuse author with narrator.
16. Usually the third person. You can have a third-person omniscient all-seeing narrator.
17. Any of the ways set out on 'What to Look for in Characters' on page 76 will do for this answer.
18. An all-knowing author, usually in third-person stories.
19. Round characters develop because they change in the course of the novel. Flat characters do not change, thus they do not develop.

20. 'Conversation'. Two people speaking.
21. Dialogue makes characters vivid and lifelike. What characters say reveal their motives and personality traits; readers can learn about characters from what other characters say about them.
22. New speaker, new line and indent; begin with a capital letter; introduce with a punctuation mark and use inverted commas.
23. A character speaking alone.
24. The answer is similar to question 21. Look at the last two points of the answer to question 21.

Themes, Atmosphere and the Differences between Novels and Stories

25. Both have: plots, stories, dialogue, characters, themes and ideas.
26. Stories are shorter and tend to concentrate on an incident and have a shorter time-span for the action; there are also fewer characters with less detail; short stories tend to have one plot and fewer themes. Their dialogue is more fragmented. Description in short stories is more economical.
27. There is not enough space to do otherwise.
28. Through description; the use of imagery; through variety in language and sentences and through the tone of the narrator and his or her closeness to the action.
29. The choice of words chosen by the author.
30. True.
31. True.
32. False.
33. Alliteration is the repetition of initial consonants in words for an effect; assonance is the repetition of similar vowel sounds in words for an effect.
34. The main idea or message of a story.
35. Any sensible idea will be good enough here. Look again at 'Themes' on page 78 to see an example with *Roll of Thunder Hear My Cry*.
36. Check your answer by comparing novels and stories on page 83. If you've mentioned a few of them give yourself the mark.

Text Credits: Extract from 'Superman and Paula Brown's New Snowsuit' ©Sylvia Plath, by kind permission of the Estate of Sylvia Plath and Faber and Faber; Extract from 'Flight' from 'The Habit of Loving' ©1954 Doris Lessing. Reprinted by kind permission of Jonathan Clowes Ltd., London, on behalf of Doris Lessing; 'Six O'Clock News', from 'Unrelated Incidents', ©Tom Leonard, by kind permission of Tom Leonard; 'Half-Caste', from 'Get Back Pimple', ©John Agard, by kind permission of JohnAgard c/o Caroline Sheldon Literary Agency, published by Viking Puffin, 1996. Photo credits: Yoda, ©Lucasfilm/ Everett (EVT), Rex Features; Film scene from 'Othello' By Oliver Parker ©Konow Rolf/Corbis Sygma.